Theater and Incarnation

Theater and Incarnation

Max Harris

William B. Eerdmans Publishing Company
Grand Rapids, Michigan / Cambridge, U.K.

First published 1990 by Macmillan, London

This edition published 2005 by
Wm. B. Eerdmans Publishing Co.

Wm. B. Eerdmans Publishing Co.
255 Jefferson Ave. S.E., Grand Rapids, Michigan 49503 /
P.O. Box 163, Cambridge CB3 9PU U.K.

Printed in the United States of America

10 09 08 07 06 05   7 6 5 4 3 2 1

Library of Congress Cataloging-in-Publication Data

Harris, Max, 1949-
Theater and incarnation / Max Harris.
p. cm.
Originally published: New York: St. Martin's Press, 1990.
Includes bibliographical references and index.
ISBN-10 0-8028-2837-X / ISBN-13 978-0-8028-2837-8 (pbk.: alk. paper)
1. Theater — Religious aspects — Christianity. 2. Religion and drama.
3. Incarnation in literature. I. Title.

PN2049.H27 2005
809.2′9382321 — dc22

2005050752

www.eerdmans.com

Contents

Preface

E. H. Gombrich, in *Art and Illusion,* makes the now celebrated point that an artist attempting to "copy" what he sees is influenced as much by prior "copies" as he is by the object under observation. He gives as an example Dürer's drawing in 1515 of a rhinoceros, dependent in large measure on the stylized images of dragons found in medieval bestiaries. Even more striking is Heath's engraving of a rhinoceros in 1789. Although announced as "designed from life" and based on first-hand observation, the illustration clearly bears a greater resemblance to Dürer's drawing than it does to the photograph of a rhinoceros placed beside it. Convention is a lens that shapes the world we see.[1]

This is no less true for the critic. S. L. Bethell has remarked that "critics who think themselves disinterested" are actually "the least impartial," being "swayed unconsciously by the beliefs they have necessarily acquired by being members of a particular society in a particular place and time." Try as we may for "neutrality," we all write from within a tradition and from a particular perspective, and it is best to be as honest as possible about that viewpoint from the outset. That way, the critic, "if not entirely avoiding prejudice, may at least give his readers fair warning of what to expect."[2] I own, therefore, that I write from

1. E. H. Gombrich, *Art and Illusion* (Princeton: Princeton University Press, 2nd edn., 1961) pp. 81-82.

2. S. L. Bethell, *Essays on Literary Criticism and the English Tradition* (London: Dennis Dobson, 1948) p. 25.

within the Christian tradition. My "seeing" of things is permeated — obscured or illuminated, depending on your viewpoint — by my encounter with the person of Jesus Christ as I find him in the pages of Scripture. It is probably saturated with a great deal else as well, but this will do for a start.

Many viewpoints, though, shelter under the umbrella of Christianity and it may be helpful to specify my own particular bias further, not in the form of confessional statement, but in terms of the particular issues at stake in the discussion of theater and religion that follows. Nathan Scott has proposed that "the great effort of the Christian critic in our day should no doubt have as its ultimate aim a reconciliation between the modern arts and the Church, between the creative imagination and the Christian faith." But he recognizes that "immense obstacles" lie in the path of such an achievement, not the least of which is the perception among so many at the forefront of modern art that Christianity is a matter of asceticism and of retreat from the passions and possessions of this world that form the material of art. It is often felt, in the words of Amos Wilder, "that a Christian so sterilizes his heart that there is no concern left for art and the rich play, the riot and fecundity of life."[3]

Neither Scott nor Wilder share this view of Christ as ascetic. Nor do I, and I consider it strange that a faith grounded in the conviction that the divine Word became, of all things, flesh, should pose as ascetic. But it is undeniable that Christianity has, "at sundry times and in divers manners," presented just such a wan and haggard face to the world. It seems to me, however, that the root of such a persistent tendency to otherworldliness lies not in the dramatic entry of God into the world which I see at the heart of the Christian *kerygma* but in a kind of Gnosticism or neo-Platonism which seeks to escape from the world and which has often found too fertile soil in the Church. Of this we will say more later. For now, we introduce the theater.

Theater has a hard time being ascetic. It may drift towards ritual and it may flirt with abstraction but, except in short-lived experiment and the dreams of a visionary like Mallarmé, its medium is flesh, the

3. N. A. Scott, Jr., *Negative Capability* (New Haven, Conn.: Yale University Press, 1969) pp. 139-41; A. N. Wilder, *The Spiritual Aspects of the New Poetry* (New York: Harper, 1940) pp. 197-98.

flesh of the actor or actress who is, together with the audience, the irreducible minimum beyond which theater disappears. To put it another way, theater is a determinedly sensory medium, engaging in varying degree all the senses of the audience and not just, for example, the sight of the reader or the hearing of the listener. If, as Scott and Wilder suggest, art resists asceticism, then theater, as the fleshiest, most sensual and, in the view of a long parade of ecclesiastical critics from the Church Fathers to the Puritans and Fundamentalists, the most "worldly" of art forms, does so more vigorously than any other medium. It is therefore a fine vantage point from which to take the "ultimate aim" that Scott proposes to "the Christian critic in our day." If the Incarnation and theater can be not merely reconciled but shown, in some sense, to be paradigms of one another, then a significant advance may be made towards "a reconciliation . . . between the creative imagination and the Christian faith." It is this that I propose: that the idea of the Incarnation is through and through theatrical, and that the theater, at its most joyous, occupies common ground with the Incarnation in its advocacy of what Karl Barth has called "the good gift of [our] humanity."[4]

I begin by suggesting that theatrical texts should be read not as finished works of "literature" but as "scores" for performance (ch. 1) and therefore with due regard for the simultaneously temporal and spatial dimensions of theatrical performance (ch. 2). I then argue that, whatever may be true of poetry, theater does not generate a self-contained aesthetic world but imitates or denotes a world beyond performance (ch. 3) and addresses and aims to influence a particular human audience (ch. 4). In each of these chapters, I propose that what may be said of the theater may also be said, *mutatis mutandis,* of God's mode of self-revelation as it was understood by the writers of Scripture. Biblical text points to divine act, which, it is claimed, makes known the character of God and his creation and does so in human signs and before human audiences. At times, therefore, a "theatrical hermeneutic" may offer the most fruitful way of reading Scripture.

In the latter half of the book, I consider the range of evaluative stance taken by the theater towards "the riot and fecundity of life" off stage, whether it be one of celebration or escape (ch. 5), of fastidious de-

4. K. Barth, *The Humanity of God* (Richmond, Va.: John Knox Press, 1960) p. 54.

corum or raucous and merciful embrace (ch. 6). Such a stance, I suggest, is also apparent in the various relationships proposed in the theater between seen and unseen worlds (ch. 7), and, perhaps most emphatically, in the vantage point from which the theater addresses the problem of conflict and the hope of resolution (ch. 8). In these chapters, I am interested in the degree to which theater, often in the most unexpected places, does or does not endorse what I understand to be the testimony of the Incarnation to the value of the flesh and of human time and space as a proper dwelling place for God and therefore for humankind.

For the sake of theological consistency, I have chosen not to use a myriad of theologians to represent "Christianity" but, for the most part, one: Karl Barth. There is both reason and mischief in this. First the reason: among modern theologians, Barth has more than any other made the Word becoming flesh the centerpiece of his theology. Secondly, the mischief: Barth has been presumed by many to have adopted an entirely negative stance towards culture and to have declared all the best efforts of humanity to be riddled with unbelief. That he should nonetheless have so appreciated Mozart is a puzzle to those who see him in this light, but not enough of a puzzle to shake their conviction. But not all view Barth this way. John Updike, introducing a volume of Barth's thoughts on Mozart, wrote:

> Karl Barth's insistence upon the otherness of God seemed to free him to be exceptionally (for a theologian) appreciative and indulgent of this world, the world at hand. His humor and love of combat, his capacity for friendship even with his ideological opponents, his fondness for tobacco and other physical comforts, his tastes in art and entertainment were heartily worldly not in the fashion of those who accept this life as a way-station and testing-ground but of those who embrace it as a piece of Creation.[5]

To use Barth's theology as a fruitful tool for the unpacking of the relationships between the theater and the Incarnation would not only confirm Updike's perception but provide a certain mischievous satisfaction. A previous attempt to describe Barth's "theology of culture" was

5. J. Updike, "Foreword," in K. Barth, *Wolfgang Amadeus Mozart,* trans. C. K. Pott (Grand Rapids, Mich.: Eerdmans, 1986) p. 7.

introduced with the remark, "[the author] certainly knows how to arouse curiosity: a theology of culture by Barth? How is such a square peg going to fit a round hole?"[6] There is a measure of playful delight in showing that the peg may in fact be round, or, to use the illustration with which we began, to reveal an alternative, if not yet the real, rhinoceros hiding behind the stereotype.

It is impossible to thank in print all who have helped to shape the character of an author or the ideas that issue in a particular book. I would like first, therefore, to thank all those whose names will not appear below but who nonetheless, as teachers, colleagues and friends over the years, have contributed more than they can know to my own growth or to the formation of this book.

Among those who have contributed to my formal education, it is appropriate here to thank especially those who shared and encouraged my interest in medieval drama: Richard Axton, John Elliott, Del Kolve and Bob Potter. Outside the academic arena, I want to thank all those who engaged in theatrical experiment with me in student days, particularly but not exclusively three very good friends, Walter Davis, Michael Kuhn and John Sedgwick. For nurturing my faith, I owe a special debt to Jerram Barrs, Clive Boddington, Ranald Macaulay and their families. Larry Bouchard, Ann Harris, Nathan Scott and Lael Woodbury have read the present manuscript in whole or in part, and I am grateful to them for their encouragement and suggestions for improvement. David Jasper has been an invaluable asset in his gentle and careful critique of my manuscript in its various stages.

Finally, to my wife, Ann, to my children, Joel and Matthew, to my parents, John and Betty, and to my sister, Julie, I owe thanks that words cannot express. For from them I have received patient and faithful love.

M.H.

6. H. M. Rumscheidt, "Foreword," in R. J. Palma, *Karl Barth's Theology of Culture* (Allison Park, Penn.: Pickwick Publications, 1983) p. vii.

Chapter 1 Text and Performance

The playwright Peter Shaffer prefaced an edition of his *Collected Plays* with an appeal to the reader to use his theatrical imagination:

> These pages seem to me to resemble those Japanese toy shells which, dropped into a tumbler of water, release a string of colored flowers. My water is the atmosphere of a theater. The more the reader can supply that for himself, the more he will see the plays released from their shells of paper and expand into their full life and colors.[1]

This is a good place to begin a consideration of the theater. For it is all too easy to forget that dramatic texts, unlike most poems or novels, are incomplete works of art, "scores for speech and action whose final artistic life is only suggested on the manuscript page";[2] in short, that a transformation is effected when words are staged.

It is also a good place to begin a consideration of the relationship between religion and the theater. For something akin to the transformation of text into performance is found at the very heart of the Christian faith. The proclamation that "the Word became flesh" (Jn. 1:14)[3]

1. P. Shaffer, *The Collected Plays of Peter Shaffer* (New York: Harmony, 1982) p. xviii.

2. V. A. Kolve, *The Play Called Corpus Christi* (Stanford: Stanford University Press, 1966) p. 7.

3. Biblical quotations throughout, unless otherwise indicated, are from the Revised Standard Version.

suggests that speech became spectacle, that God, if you will, dropped himself incarnate into the atmosphere of the world, no longer hidden within the "shell" of what he had said or spoken into being, but seen in the flesh in his full life and color.

The author of the First Letter of John rejoiced in the abundant sensuality of the apostolic encounter with the Word. "That which was from the beginning" had now become that "which we have heard, which we have seen with our eyes, which we have looked upon and touched with our hands" (1 Jn. 1:1). In this brief passage, the writer mentions three of the five senses. The other two were not neglected: the meals that Christ shared with his disciples – the sacramental Last Supper or the practical lakeside breakfast of baked bread and fish (Jn. 21:9-13) – appealed also to human taste and smell. The Incarnation, in short, as the New Testament writers reported it, engaged all five senses.

Of all the arts, the theater alone accosts all the senses. While sight and sound ordinarily predominate, touch, taste and smell may at times play a deliberate and significant part. Actors may reach out to touch the audience; food may be shared; and, along with the unavoidable "smell of the greasepaint," there may be the soothing aroma of incense or the pungent stench of smoke accompanying battle and the melodramatic entry of the villain. If, therefore, any of the arts were to provide an apt metaphor for the revelation event to which the apostles testify, it would not be the purely literary arts of the written word, but the fully sensual art of the theater. I use the word "sensual" here not pejoratively but in its original and simple meaning of "perceptible to the senses": in both theater and, according to the classic texts of the Christian Church, in the central act of divine self-revelation, word is made manifest to the senses.

The Cornish *Ordinalia*

It may be helpful at this point to separate the two strands of theater and religion and to consider each in turn, focusing in both instances on the transformation effected when text is embodied in performance. In the case of the theater, recognition of this transformation has begun to change the way in which drama is studied. The late Neville Denny reported with approval in 1973 a marked shift of interest where drama studies are concerned from the private encounter with the printed play-text (essentially a literary interest) to the total theatrical experience for which the text exists as a properly dramatic blueprint.[4]

The development from textual blueprint to theatrical performance can be well illustrated from a production which Denny himself instigated. In 1969, at Piran Round in Cornwall, the Bristol University Drama Department, under Denny's direction, revived the fifteenth-century Cornish *Ordinalia.* The play, kin to the English Corpus Christi plays and continental Passion Plays, recounts the history of the world from its Creation to the Ascension of Christ.

The incident in which Jesus cleanses the Temple, after his triumphal entry to Jerusalem on Palm Sunday, is a good example of the transformation effected when words are staged. The text of the *Ordinalia* at this point is brief.[5] Jesus commands:

> Out, all you traders, get out! You are making a mockery of God and his holy church when you turn my house of prayer into a bazaar, into a den for loathsome thieves.

And a Trader objects:

> Say now, you there, Jesus, what token have you got for exhibiting all this muscle, giving us the back of your hand, scattering our stock hither and yon and ruining the fair?

The conversation then turns to Jesus' claim that he can affirm his authority by raising the Temple in three days should it be destroyed. The brief exchange is not immediately suggestive of spectacular theatricality.

There had been some indication earlier of the action that might accompany this verbal confrontation between Jesus and the Trader. After blessing the children who had heralded his Palm Sunday entry, Jesus had announced:

4. N. Denny, "Arena Staging and Dramatic Quality in the Cornish Passion Play," in N. Denny (ed.), *Medieval Drama* (London: Edward Arnold, 1973) p. 7.

5. For the dialogue that follows, see *The Cornish Ordinalia,* trans. Markham Harris (Washington, DC: The Catholic University of America Press, 1969) pp. 89-91.

> I will dismount and go into the Temple that I may see for myself the nature and extent of that so-called fair. If there are buyers and sellers of goods in the house of God, I will drive them out, to the last man, and overturn their wares.

And after the upheaval Pilate comments:

> What goings-on we're having in the Temple at the hands of that faker and vagabond Jesus! He's wrecked the market and is making a big thing of it because he's hungry for prestige.

These four short speeches, however, are the sum of the textual blueprint for action on this occasion.

If we are to imagine the performance to which this blueprint points, we must first have some idea of the conditions under which the *Ordinalia* was originally staged. It was by all accounts a festive event, both large-scale and popular, whose performance stretched over three days. A contemporary eye-witness remembered how, to stage the play,

> they raise an earthen amphitheatre in some open field, having the diameter of his enclosed plain some 40 or 50 foot. The country people flock from all sides, many miles off, to hear and see it.[6]

Around the circumference of the amphitheater, on top of the embankment, were placed several enclosed booth stages, called "mansions" or "scaffolds." Each represented a different location, the identity of which depended on the day's action. One, however, remained constant throughout the three days of the performance. This was "Heaven, a grand and commanding presence," populated by God and all his angels, "the dominating visual element in the entire theatrical environment." The other and opposing constant was an enormous hell-mouth, "a lividly painted, nightmare creation of fanged and gaping jaws, glaring eyes and smoking nostrils," set not on top of the embankment but at ground level in a breach in the earthen wall. Between these mansions was spread out the audience, "on tiered rows of seating capa-

6. Quoted in *The Cornish Drama,* trans. E. Norris, 2 vols. (Oxford: Oxford University Press, 1859) II, p. 453. I have, here as elsewhere, modernized medieval spelling.

ble of accommodating two or three thousand spectators." The ground level of the enclosed arena included further scenic properties and provided the main playing area. For the Palm Sunday episode one of these properties would have been the Temple, a three-dimensional "emblematic structure," establishing place but having no aspirations to strict realism.[7]

Such an earthen amphitheater survives at Piran Round, near Perranporth. It was here that Denny staged the *Ordinalia* in 1969. His intention was to remain as faithful as possible to the original methods of production; his discovery was that, as he did so, the text came alive. As text was translated by the company into performance, the action implied by the text but often overlooked in reading was uncovered.

For the dialogue to be staged intelligibly, an astonishing number of things had to happen simultaneously as the Palm Sunday entry drew near. John and Peter went to fetch the ass and, as they led it back to the little knot of disciples around Jesus, a crowd filtered in and began to line a sinuous route winding to and fro across the arena from Jesus towards the Temple. Meanwhile a bazaar was being set up in the Temple, "complete with produce, pottery, ale-jars, bolts of cloth, baskets of pigeons and (one imagines, in this region) sheep." The nobility appeared in their "mansions," wives and womenfolk, children and retainers going down to join the crowd, the men remaining on their scaffolds to survey the bustling scene below. While all this was going on, there was also visible the continued "presence of God and his angels overseeing all from the Heaven mansion, and . . . the equally telling presence, louring and malevolent, of Hell," belching forth smoke and black-clad demons into the arena.

Gradually the palm-strewn procession began to wend its way across the round. A group of "catechumens" settled down to be taught by Jesus some distance from the Temple. At the Temple itself the bazaar was in full swing. From their "houses" atop the rim of the embankment the nobility and their servants looked down on the mass of people and animals below. Then suddenly Jesus strode over to the Temple, cracked his whip and ejected the money changers and the merchants from the bazaar. Pandemonium broke loose. Goods and produce went sprawling, bolts of cloth unrolled, ale-jars spilled and shattered, sheep

7. Denny, op. cit., pp. 130-34.

scattered, pigeons exploded upwards from overturned baskets, merchants were "tumbled helter-skelter out of the way, yelling in protest but scattering as the whip crack[ed] anew, flying in all directions from the cyclonic rage within the Temple."

Denny comments:

> The point of interest is the number of things happening simultaneously over such a wide area: sheep, pigeons, fleeing chapmen, screaming women; the commanding, wrathful figure of Jesus; the startled catechumens . . . ; the equally startled ring of observers up on the embankment top. The audience's eyes must be darting everywhere, like spectators' at an ice-hockey match. In theatrical terms, the effect is electric.[8]

This comparison of the text of the *Ordinalia* with Denny's account of its performance well illustrates the transformation effected when words are staged. To the single medium of the printed word is added, in the case of the *Ordinalia,* a plethora of color and movement, costume and set, the noise and smell of animals and the music of "angels" and minstrels.

Theatrum Gloriae Dei

Literary critics must imagine or recall a performance if they are to do justice to the dramatic text they are reading. To read a play as if it were a poem, paying attention primarily to the medium of the written word, will miss much of the dramatist's art.

Something similar might be ventured of the reader of Scripture. Barth reminds us that Calvin "described the totality of the cosmos and cosmic occurrence as the *theatrum gloriae Dei,*" and comments that the work of God's grace,

> which is not an *opus ad intra* like the inner acts of the trinitarian God but most definitely an *opus ad extra,* needs outside *(extra Deum)* a theatre on which it can be enacted and unfolded. The cre-

8. For Denny's account of the Palm Sunday episode, which I have both quoted and paraphrased at length, see ibid., pp. 136-39.

> ated cosmos including man, or man within the created cosmos, is this theatre of the great acts of God in grace and salvation.[9]

As a play script bears testimony to a past or future performance, so, Barth would suggest, the Bible bears witness to God's acts of grace in "the theatre of [His] covenant."[10] This being the case, Christians who pay attention only to the medium of the written word and resist imaginative reconstruction of the very palpable events to which it claims to bear witness will miss much of the fully sensual and even theatrical nature of God's self-revelation. They will also, by implication, miss something of the nature of the Christian God, who, it may be said, chose such a mode of revelation, and of humanity, to whom God felt such a mode of revelation to be best suited.

Perhaps, in this respect, plays such as the *Ordinalia* were aids to the understanding of revelation in more ways than one. Not only did they remind the audience of the narrative of God's dealings with man, but they also helped the audience to grasp the emphatically sensual manner of the self-revelation to which that narrative testifies. Among those who, in the late Middle Ages, defended the Church's use of art for religious purposes, it was a commonplace to point out that the artist "helps men to imagine; he gives substantial form to that which is past, or to come, or invisible." The popular drama

> furnishes images too, but of a superior sort; the plays are "quike bookis," living books that speak, move, and can imitate whole sequences of events and interactions. They image more vividly and more unforgettably than any other art form of their time.[11]

The cycle plays imaged not only the story but, in their very theatricality, what was believed to be the manner of God's self-revelation.

To speak of history as the *theatrum gloriae Dei* is to speak from the perspective of faith. But the advantage of bringing a theatrical imagination to bear on the biblical text could also be maintained from a perspective of reasonable doubt. The Bible is composed of a variety of lit-

9. K. Barth, *Church Dogmatics,* trans. G. W. Bromiley *et al.,* 5 vols. (Edinburgh: T. & T. Clark, 1956-75) 3/3, pp. 47-48.

10. Ibid., 3/1, p. 99.

11. Kolve, op. cit., p. 5.

erary genres: song, parable, proverb, saga, poetic narrative, to name just a few. Some parts, however, present themselves as records of history, claiming to point beyond text to past action. Luke's gospel, for example, undertakes to be "an orderly account" of "the things which have been accomplished among us, just as they were delivered to us by those who from the beginning were eyewitnesses" (Lk. 1:1-3). One may grant that all history reaches the reader through the lens of one or more witnesses and that it is virtually impossible to reconstruct independently the actual events that lay behind the testimony. Nonetheless, the world of historical narrative is more fully entered when an effort is made to pass beyond the written word to an imaginative reconstruction of the events to which it professes to bear witness. The application of a theatrical imagination to the biblical text should not be viewed as involving a claim to unmediated reconstruction of historical events. One need think of oneself only as imagining events as they were witnessed and reported by the early Church through the lens of faith.

One can, after all, apply a theatrical imagination to a work of fiction. The difference, and the reason for the particular appropriateness of a theatrical reading in the case of the biblical text, is twofold. First, there is the matter of authorial claim. Even the most convinced skeptic will concede that whereas Cervantes, for example, does not believe that the events described in *Don Quixote* happened outside his imagination or his text, the author of Luke's Gospel was persuaded that he had recorded, as accurately as he was able, actual historical events. One enters into his world only if one imagines them as such. Secondly, the nature of the events described in the Bible is often inherently theatrical. At the heart of the narrative is the transformation of Word into flesh; much of the action entails an encounter between performer and audience; and many events are interpreted as mimetic types, "imitating" other events yet to be played.

The deliverance of God's people from captivity in Egypt is a good example of this theatricality. It is recorded both as a spectacular event of historical import in its own right, "staged" at least in part with a view to its effect on Egyptian and Israelite "spectators," and as an enacted image of future grace. The exodus was theatrical not only in its scale but in its details: the successive rounds of the "miracle plague" competition between Moses and Pharaoh's magicians; the comedy of Pharaoh's magicians summoning yet more frogs to prove that they can make life miserable too; the astonishing visual juxtaposition of devastated army and unarmed slaves; the closing triumphant dance of the Israelite women. It was theatrical too in its concern for audience, whether it be Yahweh's advance declaration that the action is designed so that the Israelites will "know that I am the LORD your God" (Ex. 6:7) and the Egyptians "may know that the earth is the LORD's" (Ex. 7:5, 9:29), or whether it be the fact that Moses and Aaron perform their miracles "before Pharoah and his servants" (Ex. 7:10). And it was theatrical finally in that it pointed beyond itself, "imitating" the future defeat of the Canaanites (Ex. 15:14-17) or, as the Christian Church has understood it, the yet greater liberation to be accomplished by Christ.

The Bible abounds in smaller instances of such theatricality. That, for instance, the invisible God stood against the rock at Horeb in front of the elders and people of Israel and allowed himself to be beaten with Moses' rod so that water might flow from the rock to assuage Israel's thirst (Ex. 17:1-6), has been interpreted as both an immediate gracious provision for material need and a carefully staged figurative enactment of Jesus' crucifixion and the consequent outpouring of the Holy Spirit (Jn. 7:37-39; cf. 1 Cor. 10:4).[12] Faced with the rebellion of his people, God played the part of the criminal and was punished in their stead; blessings flowed.

In the Old Testament one thinks also of the ceremonies of the tabernacle and temple, assaulting the senses with the force of a butcher's shop and a papal Mass combined, and yet all of them in one way or another enacting dramatic witness to the coming "Lamb of God," who would "take away the sins of the world" (Jn. 1:29). One thinks of the street theater of the prophets; of Isaiah going "naked and barefoot for three years as a sign" that the invading "king of Assyria" would "lead away the Egyptians captives and the Ethiopians exiles, both the young and the old, naked and barefoot, with buttocks uncovered" (Is. 20:1-6); or of Ezekiel making a clay model of Jerusalem and enacting a mock-siege against it, complete with siegeworks, mound and battering rams, as "a sign for the house of Israel" (Ezek. 4:1-3), warning of imminent

12. C. H. McIntosh, *Notes on the Book of Exodus* (Chicago: Fleming H. Revell, 1873) pp. 222-24; E. P. Clowney, *Preaching and Biblical Theology* (Grand Rapids: Eerdmans, 1961) p. 79.

judgement. History, ceremonies and prophetic utterances, though recorded in written word, were acted in theatrical medium.

All this, as the New Testament interprets it, was preparation for the central act of God's self-revelation in Christ. When "the Word became flesh," there was present on the stage of history "the image of the invisible God" (Col. 1:15), one who was "the radiance of God's glory and the exact representation of his being" (Heb. 1:3 NIV). The fourth Gospel proclaims that in Christ the otherwise hidden God has fully made himself known. Well aware of the Old Testament revelation, the evangelist yet announces, "No one has ever seen God; the only Son, who is in the bosom of the Father, he has made him known" (Jn. 1:18). The full extent of that revelation in Christ is declared most forcefully in the use of the word "truth" in the same passage. We read, "The Word became flesh and dwelt among us, full of grace and truth; we have beheld his glory, glory as of the only Son from the Father"; and again, "For the law was given through Moses; grace and truth came through Jesus Christ" (Jn. 1:14, 17). John Murray comments on this passage in his book *Principles of Conduct:*

> It is to miss the thought entirely to suppose that truth is here contrasted with the false or the untrue. The law was not false or untrue. What John is contrasting here is the partial, incomplete character of the Mosaic dispensation with the completeness and fulness of the revelation of grace and truth in Jesus Christ. . . . The Mosaic revelation was not destitute of grace and truth. But grace and truth in full plenitude came by Jesus Christ.[13]

The distinction Murray is making can be illustrated in terms of the oath taken by a witness in court. Swearing to tell the truth, the witness further defines his promise in two ways: he swears to tell "the whole truth" and "nothing but the truth." The former phrase commits him to withhold no information; the latter phrase commits him to tell no falsehood. The author of the fourth Gospel is using the word "truth" in the former sense. Though Moses revealed no falsehood, Christ embodied "the whole truth" about God. When the divine Word costumed himself in human flesh and dwelt among men, he also, to reverse the

13. J. Murray, *Principles of Conduct* (Grand Rapids: Eerdmans, 1957) p. 123.

theatrical metaphor, unmasked himself. The subject of all previously enacted images was no longer hidden in ceremonies and figurative history but present among men, fully accessible to their senses. "The whole truth" walked the dusty stage.

The one who "made God known" in this way was a consummate performer. Joachim Jeremias, among others, has insisted that Jesus' parables were occasional pieces of performance told to and often "intended to startle" specific audiences.[14] At times Jesus played one segment of his audience against another. Pharisees and followers mixed in Jesus' Passion Week audiences: the Pharisees understood that the parables of Passion Week were told against them, but were unable to arrest Jesus in the presence of enthusiastic "multitudes" (Matt. 21:45-46). Jeremias adds that "Jesus did not confine himself to spoken parables, but also performed parabolic actions."[15] As he approached Jerusalem by way of Jericho, amidst speculation among his followers as to who was to participate and who was to rule in the coming kingdom, he welcomed children the disciples had turned away, turned away a rich and pious young ruler the disciples would have welcomed, healed a blind beggar the crowd was trying to silence and dined with Zacchaeus who was rich but unpopular (Lk. 18:15–19:10). Audience expectation as to status in the kingdom was turned topsy-turvy by these successive "parabolic actions."

The New Testament also suggests the presence of an unseen audience. Commenting on the multitude of angels viewing "a Lamb, standing as though it had been slain," and in song ascribing worth to the Lamb for his work of redemption (Rev. 5:6-10), Karl Barth proposes that the angels are viewing "the event which took place on earth . . . on Golgotha, before the gates of Jerusalem."[16] Other passages, Eph. 3:10 and 1 Cor. 4:9 among them, speak of an angelic audience. The latter is particularly germane, since there Paul describes human activity before a vast audience as "theater." "Paul tells us," Barth comments, "that the apostles are made a θέατρον to the cosmos and angels and men."[17]

Theatricality extends beyond the New Testament into the ongo-

14. J. Jeremias, *The Parables of Jesus,* trans. S. H. Hooke (New York: Scribner's, 1962) p. 36.

15. Ibid., p. 227.

16. Barth, *CD,* 3/3, p. 473.

17. Ibid., p. 500.

ing life of the Church. The sacraments, instituted by Christ, appeal to all the senses. In the Eucharist, for example, when incense is wafted and richly brocaded vestments are worn, the senses of smell and sight are abundantly gratified; and even in those traditions that emphasize the preaching of the word and simplicity of style, there is still dramatic enactment. The hearing of the word and the singing of hymns, the sight of bread being broken and wine being poured, the touch of loaf and cup against fingers and lips, the scent and taste of the elements, and perhaps the embrace or handshake of fellow worshippers; these are the sensual constituents of the Supper. Here, as with Old Testament Israel and, centrally, in the Incarnation, the Christian God may be understood to have declared his commitment to a fully theatrical and not merely verbal mode of addressing his people.

Theatrical Hermeneutics

If, as I have suggested, there is a transformation effected when word becomes performance and, in reverse, when performance is encoded in text, and if, as I have also suggested, the Christian concept of God's mode of self-revelation is theatrical, then the sensitive reader of script and Scripture alike will need to engage in a form of theatrical hermeneutics that both animates and interprets text.

In a sense this is true of any encounter with a text. "Consider," writes Richard Palmer in *Hermeneutics,* "the act of reading aloud":

> Oral interpretation is not a passive response to the signs on the paper like a phonograph playing a record; it is a creative matter, a performance, like that of a pianist interpreting a piece of music.

Just as the musical score is a "mere shell," so the printed text is "a mere husk of the original – 'outlines' of the sounds without indications of pitch, emphasis, and attitude," which the reader must interpret and present "in living sound." Palmer goes on to suggest that "every silent reading of a literary text is a disguised form of oral interpretation":

> A literary criticism which aspires to be an "enabling act" is in part an effort to make up for the weakness and helplessness of the written word; it tries to put back in the work the dimensions of speech.

A critic hearing an oral recitation of a sonnet compares it "with his own imagined performance." Confronting the same sonnet in writing he searches for "other written words . . . to replace what was lost" in the transition from real or imagined performance to text. He tries to supply, in written description, something of "what a good oral interpretation supplies in the medium of pure sound." Palmer concludes therefore that "an adequate literary criticism moves toward the oral interpretation of the work on which it is focused."[18]

Now, if this is true of the reading of a sonnet, which presupposes only performance in the medium of sound, how much more is it true of the reading of a play text or portion of Scripture that presupposes "performance" in the multimedia of stage or the *theatrum gloriae Dei.* The critic, by an act of the imagination, must seek to "put back into the work the dimensions" of sound, color, movement, speech, taste, smell and touch lost in the transition to written text or awaiting release in future performance.

Medieval plays like the Cornish *Ordinalia* exercised just such a theatrical hermeneutic on the biblical narrative. However, as the *Ordinalia* well illustrates, when these missing dimensions are restored to the text by way of theatrical performance they bear with them a distinctly local and contemporary flavor. Not only is the language translated, first, in the case of the *Ordinalia,* into Cornish and then, for Denny's production, into modern English, but historical details and geographical locale are also translated. Caiaphas, for example, becomes a "bishop," Pilate a "magistrate" and the Roman soldiers and Temple guard coalesce as "torturers" with a characteristically Cornish enthusiasm for "wrestling."[19]

Such contemporaneity is arguably inherent to the theater. The flexibility of live performance allows and the presence of a live audience demands contemporaneity of reference. Theater audiences, like church congregations, rarely consist of antiquarian scholars: they demand that the text speak today. And so the *Ordinalia* translated biblical story into contemporary and local theater. What is more, a play script is much less precise than an architectural blueprint, serving more to

18. R. E. Palmer, *Hermeneutics* (Evanston: Northwestern University Press, 1969) pp. 16-18.

19. *The Cornish Ordinalia,* pp. 91, 155.

suggest possible performances than to delineate a single option. There is, in other words, more than one possible performance to which the textual blueprint points, and the nature of a particular performance will be shaped as much by the interests and outlook of the players and of the audience for which it is performed as it will be by the text. To use the language of Hans-Georg Gadamer, theatrical performance involves in some measure a "fusion of two" or even three "horizons," the horizon or "world" of the text and those, not necessarily identical, of its performers and audience.[20]

Mysteries for Today

The variety of performances that can be mounted from a single text, as well as the contemporaneity of theatrical hermeneutics, can be illustrated by comparing the Bristol University production of the *Ordinalia* with another modern performance of medieval drama. The 1985 National Theatre production of *The Mysteries,* a conflation of texts from several of the medieval Corpus Christi plays, told the story of the world from Creation to Doomsday. While Neville Denny's insights into the text of the *Ordinalia* derived in great part from his faithfulness to medieval staging methods, *The Mysteries* tried "to reproduce the startling effect the plays would have had on their original audience by presenting them in an aggressively demotic modern setting."[21] Put another way, what the medieval text of the *Ordinalia* did to the biblical narrative, the 1985 production of *The Mysteries* did to the medieval play texts.

The Corpus Christi texts are as strongly flavored by their own time and place as is the text of the *Ordinalia.* Cain complains of having to tithe to the parish priest; devils travel to Doomsday "up Watling Street"; and the shepherds who visit the Christ child are indistinguishable, in dialect, costume and frame of reference, from the shepherds who would have been found in their fifteenth-century north Yorkshire audience. Such contemporaneity can be given due weight in perfor-

20. H.-G. Gadamer, *Truth and Method* (New York: Seabury Press, 1975) p. 273.

21. H. O'Donoghue, "Arresting Anachronisms," *Times Literary Supplement,* 1 February 1985, p. 121. In my account of *The Mysteries* that follows, I quote also from the reviews of A. Franks, I. Wardle and B. Levin in, respectively, the 18, 21 January and 19 April editions of the *Times.*

mance by remaining faithful to the medieval setting and allowing the members of the audience to register the temporal and geographical anachronisms. This was the option Denny chose. Or one can update the performance so that its language and action is borrowed from that of the modern audience. This was the option chosen by Bill Bryden, director of the National Theatre production.

The Corpus Christi plays were originally staged by members of the local trade guilds. Bryden brought this up to date by hanging emblems of craft and labor from the balconies and huge trade union banners from the roof of the theater. The actors were dressed as twentieth-century miners and bus conductors, all with broad Yorkshire accents. God the Father descends not from a booth stage Heaven on top of the rim of an earthen embankment but from a fork-lift truck, "in a foreman's cap with a pencil tucked behind his ear, to give Noah . . . the basics on boat-building"; the Virgin Mary mourns at the foot of the cross, "a homely, plucky, working-class widow, dressed in her best coat and clutching a handbag and a crumpled paper handkerchief."

Audience involvement, another common feature of popular medieval drama, is also modernized. When Mak, the bad shepherd, is caught stealing sheep, he is not tossed in a blanket as the medieval text suggests, but made to put his head through a hole "in one of those seaside joke-photograph devices," while "the children in the audience . . . are invited to pelt him with wet sponges." More frighteningly, as Doomsday approaches, the audience among whom the action is taking place "has to be pretty agile to avoid being run over by God's fork-lift truck, or Beelzebub's dust cart [Hell]," into which not only "wicked souls" but at least one "apparently innocent theatregoer" are peremptorily manhandled. "We've tried," Bryden said, "to create, in a modern world, the sort of basis on which those original performances occurred."

Might the reader of Scripture be encouraged to exercise a similar creative freedom? Contemporaneity, as the popular medieval theater recognized, is part and parcel of the biblical witness. Though historical events are recorded, we are reminded by Paul that "they were written down for our instruction" (1 Cor. 10:11). Again, in the midst of a lengthy exegesis of Psalm 95, the writer to the Hebrews reminds his readers that the written "word of God" continues "living and active, . . . discerning the thoughts and intentions" of their hearts no less perceptively than it did those who first heard the psalm "through David." "Today," David wrote, "when you hear [the Spirit's] voice, do not harden your hearts" in response; and the writer to the Hebrews urges his readers to "exhort one another every day, as long as it is called 'today,'" to the same end (Heb. 3:7, 13; 4:7, 12). The Spirit, it is maintained, addresses God's people through Scripture "today."

Karl Barth comments:

> The Word which entered the world objectively in revelation, which was spoken once for all into the world, now wills to speak further in the world, i.e., to be received and heard in further areas and ages of the world.

Without jeopardizing the unique nature of the original and "objective" revelation, he is yet able to add, "Pietism is quite right. We speak of real revelation only when we speak of the revelation which is real for us."[22]

The medieval dramatists shaped their plays so as to speak a biblical word into a contemporary world. The merchants and money-changers in the Temple became, in the *Ordinalia,* traders at a Cornish country fair; and in modernized revival of *The Mysteries,* the Virgin Mary wears wellington boots and dries her eyes with paper tissues. While only the most naive audience would suppose that Jewish merchants dressed and spoke like medieval Cornishmen, or that Jesus' mother had the mannerisms of a working-class British housewife, it is surely in keeping with the spirit of biblical contemporaneity to engage in imaginative reconstruction of this sort. Theatrical proclamation of *kerygma* is not historical research, valid as that scholarly discipline may be. But the two may complement one another. Jeremias, like Denny, endeavors to recover "the original historical setting";[23] the medieval playwrights, like Bryden, tried to speak the dramatic word into a particular local and contemporary setting.

What the medieval playwright and director could do on stage, any reader of the Bible can do in his imagination. An Indian railway worker might imagine Jesus and his disciples travelling third-class on a crowded train and, at one of those lengthy unscheduled stops in the middle of nowhere, multiplying curry and mangoes to feed the hungry

22. Barth, *CD,* 1/2, pp. 223, 237.

23. Jeremias, op. cit., p. 38.

who have gathered to hear him speak. Or a New York City prostitute might imagine Jesus speaking to her gently on 42nd Street, in the midst of neon and pornographic display, and seeing in his eyes affection, not lust. While there is a single historical series of events to which Scripture claims to bear witness, there are as many possible imaginative reconstructions in the language of "today" as there are individuals, or at the very least cultures and sub-cultures, willing to imagine. Such creative imagining makes no pretence of meeting the rigorous standards of historical research, but it may help the reader to hear anew in his or her own time the word spoken by the Spirit of Christ.

Indeed, as James Barr has recently reminded us, "a literary, dramatic and philosophical" principle of interpretation may have certain advantages over an "historical" approach. He cites the case of the nineteenth-century Anglican scholar Benjamin Jowett, who, as "a lover of the drama,"

> certainly did not suppose that the way to understand and enjoy Shakespeare's *Macbeth* was to "reconstruct the historical reference," whether that means the sources drawn upon by the dramatist, the historical circumstances of Shakespeare's writing the play, or the historical realities of ancient Scotland (if any) that were embedded in the plot. On the contrary, though he would never have thought of expressing it in this way, it is *the text itself* that communicates meaning.

Applying this to the Scripture, as he did in his *Commentary* on selected Pauline Letters or in his celebrated essay, "On the Interpretation of Scripture," Jowett insisted that the Bible be read "like any other book," that is, as Barr explains it, with primary concentration on "the text itself."[24]

But a play script is not read "like any other book"; it is read with a view to the variety of performances it suggests. Scholarly research into the nature of the original performance may facilitate lively theatrical reading. So may attention to the horizon of a modern audience. We have seen how two very similar texts, the Cornish *Ordinalia* and the English Corpus Christi plays, gave rise to two very different performances.

24. J. Barr, "Jowett and the Reading of the Bible 'Like Any Other Book,'" *Horizons in Biblical Theology,* vol. 5, no. 1 (June 1983) pp. 7-8.

The difference lay not in the texts, but in the manner of production; it would be perfectly possible to modernize the *Ordinalia* in the manner of the National Theatre production and to produce the texts underlying *The Mysteries* in an "authentic" medieval style. Both approaches, done well, would provide further illumination of the texts. The point is simply that the sensitive reader of a dramatic text will imagine performance, and not merely one performance but a number of possible performances.

Jowett's advice should perhaps therefore be modified to suggest that the narrative portions of scripture be read "like any other dramatic text." The sensitive reader of Scripture will imagine as best he can both the specific event, in all its divinely staged theatricality, to which the Scripture testifies; and also that history transposed into his own immediate vernacular and costume. To paraphrase Peter Shaffer, one might say that such an imagination is the atmosphere into which the Scripture must be dipped if it is to be released from its shell of paper and expand into its full life and color. Of such a mode of reading, the medieval plays of salvation history provide powerful illustration and precedent.

Chapter 2 Time and Space

That the study of drama requires an approach that is distinct from the study of other literary forms becomes even clearer when one considers what Jonas Barish has provocatively called the theater's "licentious ways with time and space."[1] For, while the plastic arts occupy space and the narrative arts time, the theater makes free and simultaneous use of both. To translate dramatic text into performance, therefore, is to pass from the single temporal dimension of reading to the simultaneously temporal and spatial dimensions of performance; and what the director does on stage, the reader must do in his imagination.

That the Word became flesh, moving through human space and time, and not word, yielding his sense to the reader one cluster of letters at a time, is inherent to the doctrine of the Incarnation. A theatrical imagination, as I have suggested, may help to retrieve something of the sensual character of such an event. That a theatrical hermeneutic, sensitive to the concurrent use of space and time on stage, may generate insight into biblical passages that have remained opaque to more conventional approaches is a possibility also worth exploring.

1. J. Barish, *The Anti-theatrical Prejudice* (Berkeley: University of California Press, 1981) p. 136.

Lessing, Shakespeare and the Wedding at Cana

Lessing's classic essay of 1766, *Laocoön,* was one of the first to bring to critical attention the distinction between spatial and temporal arts. Lessing earned his early reputation as a playwright and drama critic and continued active in the theater throughout his career. But in *Laocoön* he turned his attention to the distinction between, on the one hand, the narrative art of epic poetry and, on the other, the plastic arts of sculpture and painting. The latter, he observed, employ "figures and colours in space"; the former employs "articulated sounds in time" (ch. 16).[2] That is to say, the plastic arts occupy space; temporally they are static. The narrative arts, such as poetry (and more recently the novel), occupy time; spatially they are negligible, pages of a text at most.

To illustrate his thesis, Lessing compared the classical Greek sculpture in which the priest, Laocoön, and his two sons are locked in mortal combat with a writhing serpent to Virgil's description of the same event in the *Aeneid.* Captured spatially in the marble sculpture is a single moment in time. One of the sons reaches down to try to disentangle his foot from the serpent's coils, the serpent itself is about to sink its fangs into the priest's hip, and Laocoön braces himself, with an agonized facial expression, against the bite that, in the sculpture, never comes.

In Virgil's poem, the narrative extends through time a sequential account of the struggle:

> Two giant arching sea-snakes swam over the calm waters from Tenedos, breasting the sea together and plunging towards the land. Their fore-parts and their blood-red crests towered above the waves; the rest drove through the ocean behind, wreathing monstrous coils, and leaving a wake that roared and foamed. And now, with blazing and blood-shot eyes and tongues which flickered and licked their hissing mouths, they were on the beach. We paled at the sight and scattered; they forged on, straight at Laocoön. First each snake took one of his two little sons, twined round him, tightening, and bit, and devoured the tiny limbs. Next they seized

2. G. E. Lessing, *Laocoön,* trans. E. A. McCormick (Baltimore: Johns Hopkins Press, 1984).

> Laocoön, who had armed himself and was hastening to the rescue; they bound him in the giant spirals of their scaly length, twice round his middle, twice round his throat; and still their heads and necks towered above him. His hands strove frantically to wrench the knots apart. Filth and black venom drenched his priestly hands. His shrieks were horrible and filled the sky.[3]

Virgil's account illustrates the fact that, as Lessing observed:

> There is nothing to compel the poet to compress his picture into a single moment. . . . Each [sequential] variation which would cost the artist a separate work costs the poet but a single pen stroke. (ch. 4)

It would, in other words, have taken a whole series of sculptures to portray all that Virgil can report in a mere 24 lines of poetry.

There are always exceptions testing the boundaries of any definition. One thinks in this instance of kinetic sculpture, in which moving parts form sequences of spatial arrangements, or of *poésie concrète,* in which the spatial distribution of words on the page is as important as the meaning of the words read in sequence. But though it is true, as Hazard Adams remarks, that "modern art raises new questions about the relation of temporal activity to static representation,"[4] Lessing's distinction remains pertinent.

For when, in this context, we return to dramatic texts, it is evident that a theatrical performance enjoys the best of both worlds. "Objects whose wholes or parts coexist" in space, to use Lessing's terms, are also, in the theater, "objects whose wholes or parts are consecutive" in time (ch. 16). On stage, to put it more simply, bodies occupying space move through time.

This dual range of dimensions, the concurrent employment of time and space, grants to the theater a possibility not available to other narrative arts, namely simultaneous action. In a poem or a novel, the reader is ordinarily bound to receive impressions one at a time. Thus I read in Virgil that the sea-snakes are breasting the waves; then, that

3. Virgil, *The Aeneid,* 2:199-223; trans. W. F. J. Knight (Harmondsworth: Penguin, 1958) pp. 57-58.

4. H. Adams (ed.), *Critical Theory since Plato* (New York: Harcourt Brace Jovanovich, 1971) p. 348.

with flickering tongues and hissing mouths they have landed on the beach; then, that the onlookers scatter in fear; then, that the serpents attack Laocoön's sons; and so on. No mental or optical contortions can enable me to read two sentences simultaneously. However, if this event were staged (or filmed) I would see the onlookers scatter even as I saw the serpents slither up the beach. I would hear the serpents' hissing through the human cries of terror. Laocoön and his sons would battle the snakes against a visual background of friends in flight.

The arrival of the sea-snakes would be a spectacular piece of theater. But simultaneity is not confined to spectacle. Consider a moment in Shakespeare's *Measure for Measure* when only two actors are on stage. Dressed as a friar, the Duke visits Claudio in prison and, in keeping with his clerical disguise, delivers a rambling speech of consolation in the face of death. Like many such speeches, it is full of platitudes: life is "a thing that none but fools would keep," death "no more" to be feared than "sleep." Claudio responds:

> I humbly thank you.
> To sue to live, I find I seek to die,
> And seeking death, find life: let it come on. (III. i)

Claudio's words alone do not tell us whether he is persuaded by the Duke's speech or whether his response is one of sarcastic rejection. On stage, however, the actor, in collaboration with his director, must make a decision, and by tone of voice, gesture or facial expression comment on the text even as he delivers it. The audience responds not to one element alone but to the simultaneous delivery of a number of juxtaposed elements.

A more complex example from the same play occurs in the last scene. The Duke is engaged in the public resolution of all the tangled knots of plot, uncovering hypocrisies, administering justice and ordering the weddings of already coupled pairs. In the midst of this, in front of the assembled court and people of Vienna, he proposes marriage to Isabella. He mentions it first in passing, as he pardons Claudio:

> If he be like your brother, for his sake
> Is he pardoned; and, for your lovely sake,
> Give me your hand, and say you will be mine,
> He is my brother too; but fitter time for that.

Isabella is given no chance to respond. Subsequently, the Duke is a little more direct:

Dear Isabel,
I have a motion much imports your good,
Whereto if you'll a willing ear incline,
What's mine is yours, and what is yours is mine. (V. i)

Two lines later, with no reply from Isabella, the text ends.

A major crux of interpretation for the director falls precisely at this point. In the 1979 BBC production, Isabella hesitated momentarily, but then joined hands with the Duke, and the pair led a joyous procession off stage towards his palace. Isabella had renounced the cloister and become part of the "real world"; the Duke was proclaimed the "hero" of the play. In an outdoor production in Santa Barbara, California, in 1971, Isabella reacted with shock and bewilderment, expressing facially her horrified response to the proposal. She is bound for the cloister, has spent the play fighting off Angelo's sexual advances, and is now stunned by the Duke's transformation from protector to public suitor; the Duke is confirmed as the interfering "villain" of the play.[5]

A coherent rationale can be provided for either response; ambivalence would be a third alternative. The other members of the cast must also react "in character" and in keeping with the general interpretive tenor of the production. But, one way or another, the fact that the theater employs both time and space forces the director to make a decision to which the text alone does not provide a definitive guide. Or, to put it positively, it allows him the luxury of playing the action on a number of interacting and mutually reflexive levels at the same time.

A similar distinction may be drawn between the written word of Scripture, which, in Lessing's terms, uses "signs that follow one another" (ch. 16), and the incarnate Word, who, as a living sign, would have been experienced as a simultaneous blend of human speech, action, expression and gesture, set against a background of concurrent human activity and natural setting. To remember this when engaged in imaginative reconstruction of the events reported in the biblical text can be illuminating.

5. *Measure for Measure,* directed by Max Harris, Isla Vista, California, 22 and 23 May 1971.

There is attributed to Jesus, for example, in the second chapter of John's gospel, a remark whose "apparent harshness has provoked endless discussion."[6] Together with his disciples, his mother, and a crowd of apparently very thirsty guests, Jesus was enjoying a wedding party in Cana of Galilee. Mary, perhaps noticing some consternation among the servants, said to her son, "They have no wine." On the face of it, Jesus' reply would appear to contain something of a rebuff: "O woman, what have you to do with me? [Τί ἐμοὶ καὶ σοί, γύναι;] My hour has not yet come" (Jn. 2:4).

G. H. C. Macgregor has rightly observed that "the term 'woman' in the original has none of the harshness it suggests in English," being used elsewhere (Jn. 19:26) with obvious affection.[7] Even with this qualification, however, the words that Jesus spoke to his mother remain troubling. Not only do they seem rude, but they appear to be at odds with what follows. According to the evangelist's account, Mary blithely ignored any intended rebuke and advised the servants to do whatever Jesus told them. Jesus, for his part, promptly turned some 150 gallons of water into "good wine" (Jn. 2:10).

Marcus Dods offered the interesting suggestion that Jesus' words "grate somewhat on the ear" because of "the impossibility of conveying in any words that modification of meaning which is given in the tone of voice and expression of face."[8] Is it possible that the problem of Jesus' apparent insensitivity to his mother might be resolved if we approached this text with the same kind of theatrical imagination that a director must approach a play script? If the director of *Measure for Measure* must imagine different tones of voice for Claudio's response to the Duke's piety and different facial expressions for Isabella when the Duke proposes marriage, and in each case must finally choose the one that "fits," so perhaps the reader of Scripture would do well to imagine various tones of voice, several gestures and facial expressions that might have accompanied Jesus' remark to his mother. The one that "fits" may not be the first to come to mind.

For we tend to read the words initially as if they were spoken in ir-

6. G. H. C. Macgregor, *The Gospel of John* (London: Hodder and Stoughton, 1928) p. 51.

7. Ibid.

8. M. Dods, *The Gospel of St. John* (New York: Armstrong, 1902) 2 vols., 1, p. 71.

ritation. But this requires us to explain both Jesus' "legitimate" short temper and his subsequent bounteous compliance. Commentators have shown great ingenuity in doing so.[9] One can, however, imagine a very different kind of theatrical commentary in Jesus' delivery of the text. Envisage Jesus turning to his mother with a grin on his face, a twinkle in his eye and a full cup of wine in his hand, and saying with good humour, "My good lady, what's that to us? I'm not on call right now!" (This is a colloquial but fair paraphrase of the Greek). If Mary were then to laugh, looking at her son with love and full confidence in his ebullient generosity, the exchange would have an entirely different flavor and would lead more naturally into the jovial miracle that follows.

We cannot know for certain the tone of voice and gesture that accompanied Jesus' words in this instance. The evangelist has not told us, any more than Shakespeare decreed how Claudio was to speak or Isabella to look. But, in the absence of a definitive guide, we can imagine various forms of enacted commentary until one "fits." In the case of the wedding at Cana, to imagine Jesus smiling as he speaks his line may provide the simplest elucidation of a problem text. It is not that a "literary" approach, focusing exclusively on the written word, is without value; merely that it is incomplete. A theatrical imagination, sensitive to the dimensions of simultaneous action that the text implies, is also illuminating.

Lower Depths and Spiritual Exercises

So far our examples, from both Scripture and stage, have involved the successive simultaneous action of two or more human participants. But in the theater mutual commentary can also be established between

9. K. Barth, *Erklärung des Johannes-Evangeliums (Kapitel 1–8)* (Zurich: Theologischer Verlag, 1976) p. 192, cites Calvin's view that the passage warns against the worship of Mary and Zundel's opinion that "was auf den Tisch kommt" is properly only a woman's concern! John Marsh, *Saint John* (Philadelphia: Westminster Press, 1977) p. 144, suggests that "the figure of Mary . . . may be intended to refer . . . to Judaism, . . . in whose 'womb' Jesus was conceived," but adds that Jesus was also respectfully declining "Mary's parental guidance and authority" in favor of his "relationship with his heavenly Father." He was willing to perform the miracle, not as a matter of filial obedience to Mary, but to show the transformation wrought by the presence of "the true bridegroom."

actors and technical components of the stage machinery – costume, set, lighting or recorded sound, for example – or even, in certain instances, between two or more of the technical elements alone.

Maxim Gorky's *The Lower Depths* takes place in the basement and back yard of a disreputable lodging house in the Khitrov Market area of Moscow; its occupants are tramps, both male and female, earning the rent they must pay for space in the communal basement dormitory through theft or menial labor. The setting is bleak: the opening stage direction specifies "a cavelike basement," its ceiling "blackened with smoke, with patches where the plaster has fallen off." The walls are lined with "plank beds," one of which is "screened off by a dirty cotton-print curtain," and, in the center of the room, the table, benches and battered samovar are "all unpainted and dirty."[10]

When the play was first produced, at the Moscow Art Theater in 1902 under Stanislavski's direction, the company prefaced rehearsals with a night-time expedition to the Khitrov Market and its surrounding doss-houses, on occasion having to sneak by armed gunmen to penetrate this underworld of criminals and down-and-outs. What they saw ("continuous dormitories with numberless board cots on which lay crowds of tired people that resembled corpses, – men and women") was then transferred in detail to the stage of the theater. Stanislavski's concern was for a meticulous realism of setting, costume and "local color" that would provide apt visual commentary on the dialogue and action.[11]

When, however, Erwin Piscator directed *The Lower Depths* in Berlin in 1926, he was interested not in particularity but in generalization. As a Marxist, it was important to him to place the action in the lodging-house in a broader social and historical context and to stage that context. "I could no longer think," he wrote, "in terms of a small room with ten miserable people in it, but only on the scale of the vast slums of a modern city." To achieve this effect, he began the play not in the "narrowly circumscribed" basement, but outdoors. The audience saw on stage the streets and factories of an industrial city, and heard through loudspeakers the sounds of urban dawn: "the snoring and wheezing of a crowd fills the whole stage, the city awakens, streetcar

10. M. Gorky, *The Lower Depths and Other Plays,* trans. A. Bakshy and P. S. Nathan (New Haven: Yale University Press, 1959) p. 6.

11. C. Stanislavski, *My Life in Art* (New York: Theatre Art Books, 1948) pp. 395-97.

bells ring." Only then was the focus allowed to narrow: "eventually the ceiling is lowered in and closes the room off from its surroundings." Stage machinery in this case provided the commentary not only of corroborative visual detail but of broad social context.[12]

Biblical action also takes place in a "setting." The importance of envisaging that setting, be it the immediate physical environment or the larger interpretive context, is not an exclusively "theatrical" insight. Gunkel's efforts to recover the original *"Sitz im Leben"* of the Psalms, like Jeremias' work on the "historical setting" of the parables, has greatly influenced subsequent biblical scholarship in this respect. But Gunkel and Jeremias were concerned with historical reconstruction, a discipline by which, as I have suggested, the theatrical imagination may be helped but is not bound.

A much earlier advocate of the contemplation of biblical "setting" relied more heavily on the imagination. Readers familiar with *The Spiritual Exercises of St. Ignatius* will already have noticed a similarity between what I have called "theatrical hermeneutics" and the contemplative approach to Scripture recommended by Ignatius of Loyola. Consistently he commends "seeing in imagination the persons, and . . . contemplating and meditating in detail the circumstances in which they are," as well as "hear[ing] what they are saying" (122).[13] The setting must be imagined with as much care as the action. Thus, in meditating on the Nativity, he recommends

> seeing in imagination the way from Nazareth to Bethlehem. Consider its length, its breadth; whether level, or through valleys and over hills. Observe also the place or cave where Christ is born; whether big or little; whether high or low; and how arranged. (112)

By doing so, he believes we will better appreciate the "extreme poverty" in which our Lord was born, and that this was only the beginning of the "hunger, thirst, heat, and cold, . . . insults and outrages" that culminated in his death on the cross; "and all this for me" (116).

12. E. Piscator, *The Political Theatre* (New York: Avon, 1978) pp. 119-20; cf. C. D. Innes, *Erwin Piscator's Political Theatre* (Cambridge: Cambridge University Press, 1972) p. 84.

13. *The Spiritual Exercises of St. Ignatius,* trans. L. J. Puhl (Chicago: Loyola University Press, 1951). Numerical references are to the sections.

But, like Piscator, Ignatius is also interested in the larger context. He begins his meditation on the Nativity by "calling to mind the history of the subject I have to contemplate" (102), and seeing in his mind's eye "the different persons" who form the cast of the action about to unfold:

> First, those on the face of the earth. . . . Some are white, some black; some at peace, and some at war; some weeping, some laughing; some well, some sick; some coming into the world, and some dying; . . . Secondly, I will see and consider the Three Divine Persons seated on the royal dais or throne of the Divine Majesty. They look down upon the whole surface of the earth, and behold all nations in great blindness, going down to death and descending to hell. (106)

Our Lady and the angels, the conversation of those on earth and those in heaven, the planning of divine redemption against the background of human sin, all form part of this contemplation on a grand scale.

Interestingly, in light of our observation that both theater and Incarnation are inherently "sensual," Ignatius closes his meditation on the Nativity by "applying the five senses" to the matter at hand, "seeing in imagination" the actors in the drama and the details of their circumstances, "hear[ing] what they are saying, or what they might say . . . , smell[ing] the infinite fragrance, and tast[ing] the infinite sweetness of the divinity" and, finally, "apply[ing] the sense of touch, for example, by embracing and kissing the place where the persons stand or are seated, always taking care to draw some fruit from this" (121-25). It is, one might suggest, an apt response to a "theatrical" and "sensual" mode of revelation.

One can obviously respond in this fashion to many episodes in the life of Christ or, for that matter, in the biblical narrative in general. According to Matthew, Jesus exhorted his disciples to "consider the lilies of the field" (Matt. 6:28), referring in all likelihood not to a particular species of wildflower but to the mass of spring flowers covering the Galilean hillside on which he stood.[14] If we who read are to savor the full force of the contrast between human anxiety and natural beauty,

14. W. Hendriksen, *New Testament Commentary: The Gospel of Matthew* (Grand Rapids: Baker, 1973) p. 352.

we must do as Ignatius recommends and "consider" the scene in our imagination, "applying the senses" to the evocation of wildflowers growing in effortless profusion wherever the worried disciples turn their gaze. Might we not also appreciate Christ's ministry in a different way if we were to reproduce on the mental stage of our imagination the lepers whom he touched and the underworld of prostitutes and sinners with whom he mixed in the kind of vivid detail that Stanislavski lavished on the down-and-outs of Gorky's Moscow?

As a final instance of the value of this approach, whether learned from Ignatius or from what I have been calling the exercise of a "theatrical imagination," consider the mutual commentary between human action and "stage machinery" implied in Mark's account of a storm on the Sea of Galilee. Jesus and his disciples were crossing the lake one evening in a small boat; "and a great storm of wind arose, and the waves burst into the boat, so that the boat was already filling. But [Jesus] was in the stern, asleep on the cushion" (Mark 4:37-38). If in our imagination, we place the events described by those two sentences not in temporal sequence, as they must be read, but in spatial juxtaposition in the flow of time, as the disciples experienced them, the effect is much more vivid.

We see Jesus sleeping peacefully in the stern of the boat, as the dusk sky lowers over him, the wind howls, and the boat begins to sink under the weight of water. Add what must also have been taking place at the same time, the panic of the disciples and their bellowed conferences as to whether they should wake the master, the terror on their faces and in their voices, their frantic efforts to bail out the water and to control the sails, and we have a scene of utmost confusion in the midst of which Jesus slept peacefully. Then, awakened, Jesus spoke simply to the sea, "Peace! Be still!" The wind ceased, the sky cleared, the surface of the lake was smooth, "and there was a great calm." In short, the entire "stage machinery," that a moment before was in full and frenzied swing, was instantly stilled. The disciples were stunned. It would be an extraordinary moment in the theater. It must have been all the more breathtaking in fact.

Cranfield remarks that the passage shows every sign of being "the reminiscence of an eye-witness," probably Peter. Whether we accept the text's interpretation of events or "prefer a rationalistic explanation (e.g. that the ceasing of the storm just after Jesus' words was a coincidence) will," he adds, "depend on our attitude to the miracles generally."[15] In either case, however, to re-enact the scene in imagination, paying simultaneous attention to actors and to "stage machinery," will give a more powerful sense of its original impact on the disciples. For those who accept the disciples' interpretation, theatrical imagination may rekindle awe, inspiring afresh the astonished cry, "Who then is this, that even wind and sea obey him?" (Mark 4:41).

Novel, Film and Opera

We began this chapter with Lessing's distinction between the spatial art of painting and sculpture and the temporal art of epic poetry. The theater, by contrast, employs both dimensions concurrently, breeding from its "licentious ways with space and time" that simultaneous action which is one of its characteristic delights. It will both emphasize and modify this insight if, in closing the chapter, we refer briefly to the limits of the novel and the film in this area, and, by contrast, to the freedom of the opera, which enjoys even greater liberty with space and time than its unsung theatrical cousin.

In an essay of 1945, which also began with reference to Lessing's *Laocoön,* the American critic Joseph Frank drew attention to Flaubert's attempt in the famous country fair scene from *Madame Bovary* (pt. 2, ch. 8) to create simultaneous action in the novel:

> As Flaubert sets the scene, there is action going on simultaneously on three levels. . . . On the lowest plane, there is the surging, jostling mob in the street, mingling with the livestock brought to the exhibition; raised slightly above the street by a platform are the speech-making officials, bombastically reeling off platitudes to the attentive multitudes; and on the highest level of all, from a window overlooking the spectacle, Rodolphe and Emma are watching the proceedings and carrying on their amorous conversation, in phrases as stilted as those regaling the crowds.[16]

15. C. F. B. Cranfield, *The Gospel According to Saint Mark* (Cambridge: Cambridge University Press, 1977) p. 172.

16. J. Frank, "Spatial Form in Modern Literature," in R. W. Stallman (ed.), *Critiques and Essays in Criticism* (New York: Ronald Press, 1949) p. 322.

That this attempt at simultaneity was deliberate is evident from Flaubert's own assertion, quoted by Frank, that in this scene, "Everything should sound simultaneously: one should hear the bellowing of the cattle, the whisperings of the lovers and the rhetoric of the officials all at the same time."

Interestingly, in light of our comparison with the theater, Frank recalls that the French critic Albert Thibaudet "compared this scene to the medieval mystery play, in which various related actions occur simultaneously on different stage levels." But one only has to remember the Cornish playwright's treatment of the "country fair" in the Temple on Palm Sunday and to imagine how, with his vast circular playing area and multi-level staging, he would have treated the country fair from *Madame Bovary* to realize the limitations imposed by the temporal form of the novel. Frank recognizes this handicap:

> Since language proceeds in time, it is impossible to approach this simultaneity of perception except by breaking up temporal sequence. And this is exactly what Flaubert does: he dissolves sequence by cutting back and forth between the various levels of action in a slowly-rising crescendo until — at the climax of the scene — Rodolphe's Chateaubriandesque phrases are read at almost the same moment as the names of the prize winners for raising the best pigs.[17]

But "almost" is the key word here. For all that Flaubert alternates brief snatches of the two speeches, he cannot really "dissolve sequence"; the excerpts must still be read one after another.

In the Cornish *Ordinalia,* such fragments of conversation could well have been delivered in sequence if the audience needed to hear clearly each detail. But they could also have been delivered simultaneously if, as is probably the case, only the gist of each speech needs to be grasped for the comic juxtaposition to be effective. And the ongoing presence of the actors, continuing even if momentarily silent to express themselves in gesture and facial movement, together with the background snorting and bellowing and stench of animals, the murmuring and fidgeting of the crowd and the surreptitious playing of children,

17. Ibid.

would have provided a continuity and therefore simultaneity of action not finally possible in the novel.

Film, of course, can capture simultaneous action, but not with quite the same freedom as the theater. Consider again the *Ordinalia.* The multiplicity of simultaneous action that begins with the Palm Sunday procession continues unabated through the medieval reenactment of the Passion. Judas plots with Caiaphas and Annas while Jesus concludes the Last Supper; Jesus prays in the Garden of Gethsemane while Gabriel crosses from God's scaffold to comfort him, the disciples sleep and the ambush party prepares its weapons and bolsters its courage with ale in the palace courtyard; Peter denies his master three times while Jesus is successively dragged before the high priest, interrogated and buffeted.

Visibly the action is continuous in each location. Verbally, the audience's attention is shifted from one to another by alternating snatches of dialogue. As Neville Denny points out, it is a technique akin to the sophisticated cutting from one scene to another in modern film. But, he argues, it is more than the film:

> Not even cinema, even in its "epic" wide-screen form, has been able to match, never mind excel, the dramatic possibilities, the intensities of contrast and irony and emphasis, made possible by such simultaneity of action — largely because the camera would have to move so far back (to get everything it wanted in the same sharpness of focus) that everything would be swamped in a plethora of detail. The Cornish play-makers were spared this complication. Neither were they crippled, as again the filmmakers are, by unwieldy conventions of realistic presentation. Even the wide-screen cannot contain both the courtyard [where Peter denies Christ] and the council chamber [where Jesus is interrogated] in its single view — architectural features get in the way that the Cornishmen could totally ignore.[18]

The camera can capture the broad picture and then zoom in to focus on detail. But it cannot offer both simultaneously. Nor can it happily pay equal and simultaneous attention to actions in courtyard and chamber, Gethsemane and palace. The camera, in great measure there-

18. Denny, op. cit., p. 147.

fore, determines the viewer's point of view. The theater, by contrast, because it can offer a variety of simultaneous actions, allows the spectator to select and exclude.

One particular instance of the "intensity of contrast" this freedom makes possible in the *Ordinalia* deserves further comment. During preparations for the crucifixion, the torturers responsible for securing Christ to the cross discover they have no nails and send one of their number to the smithy, on the other side of the playing area, to obtain some. The torturer and the Smith's Wife then forge nails to a dialogue that is crudely evocative of adultery. They speak of "stroking" the iron to "draw it out," and not allowing it to "go all limp and bent," of "pumping," aiming right and taking it "slow and gentle." All the while,

> at "Calvary" the preparations for the execution proceed with loud and grisly zestfulness, with Jesus and the felons being lashed to their crosses and the crowd jostling for favourable vantage points. Apart (in one of the palaces) the dignitaries relax in sociable comfort, drinking wine, exchanging pleasantries, waiting for the gala to begin.[19]

Not surprisingly, earlier commentators spoke of the "innapropriate ribaldry"[20] of the exchange between the torturer and the blacksmith's wife at this point, even while Jesus is visibly stretched on the cross. Denny tries to rescue the episode from this charge by observing that Christ's death is being shown to take place in a world like ours, and that a contrast is set up between divine love on the cross and human lust in the smithy.[21] This is true. But it seems to me that something even more sophisticated is happening.

If the scene at the smithy is played well, the audience will laugh. Popular theater audiences are notably responsive to dirty jokes. And by their laughter at the obscenity of human sin, even as Christ is dying for that sin, the spectators are themselves implicated. They have found funny the very thing for which Christ, in all seriousness, is dying. The playwright has transformed his audience from "mere spectators" to

19. Ibid., p. 152.

20. H. Jenner, "Sources of the Cornish Drama," MS. Truro Museum, Cornwall; quoted in *The Cornish Ordinalia,* p. 262.

21. Denny, op. cit., p. 153.

guilty participants even as he displays God's gracious solution to their guilt. One of the standard objections to the theater on the part of shocked Christians, be they Puritans or early Church Fathers, has been that

> "the indecencies of the spectacles . . . involve actors and audience in substantially the same guilt," for the audience, by attending and enjoying and applauding, approves, in effect, what it sees, and so shares in the sins it beholds. It is the element of spectator complicity which makes the experience perilous.[22]

The Christian playwright of the *Ordinalia* has turned this objection on its head, deliberately provoking the complicity of the audience so as to present the gospel to an audience no longer smug over its pious attendance at a religious play but convicted by its laughter at sin. It is a daring and immensely effective use of the theatrical possibilities of simultaneous action.

It is also an effect that could not have been managed so well on film. Not only would the camera have been unable to keep cross and smithy in equal and simultaneous focus. But, by focusing the viewer's attention on the low humor of the smithy to the exclusion of the cross, the camera would have shared a measure of the spectator's guilt. In the theater, though the dialogue directs the audience's attention to the bawdy, it is still the audience and not the camera that chooses where to look.

In one respect the opera has a yet greater freedom with time and space. In the conventional theater, though action may be simultaneous, speech is ordinarily successive. This is not so in opera. There is no need to explore this in detail; it can be well indicated from a single speech in Peter Shaffer's *Amadeus.* At one point, Mozart is impetuously defending his decision to write an opera based on Beaumarchais' revolutionary play, *The Marriage of Figaro.* His three pompous companions, Court Composer Salieri, Royal Chamberlain Strack and Prefect of the Imperial Library Van Swieten, are shocked. It is "a vulgar farce," unworthy of the dignity of opera. Mozart responds by springing onto a chair and declaiming, "All serious operas written this century are boring!" There follows a moment of astonished silence.

Mozart's irrepressible creativity breaks the silence:

22. Barish, op. cit., p. 80, citing Salvian, *De Gubernatione Dei,* VI, 3.

> Look at us! Four gaping mouths. What a perfect quartet! I'd love to write it — just this second of time, this *now,* as we are! Herr Chamberlain thinking, "Impertinent Mozart: I must speak to the Emperor at once!" Herr Prefect thinking, "Ignorant Mozart: debasing opera with his vulgarity!" Herr Court Composer thinking, "German Mozart: what can he finally know about music?" And Herr Mozart himself, in the middle, thinking, "I'm just a good fellow. Why do they all disapprove of me?" . . . . That's why opera is important. . . . Because it's realer than any play! A dramatic poet would have to put all those thoughts down one after another to represent this second of time. The composer can put them all down at once — and still make us hear each one of them. Astonishing device: a vocal quartet!

Mozart's point is that in a vocal quartet the concurrent thoughts of four different characters can be given simultaneous voice and, since operatic convention allows repetition, all finally be grasped by the audience. In this way a moment in real time can be isolated and explored through an extended stretch of play time. Not only can facial expression serve as commentary on speech, or action from one part of the stage remark on speech from another, as in spoken theater, but words set to music can comment on the simultaneous delivery of other words also set to music. Thought can be juxtaposed to thought in the single space created by a vocal quartet and all thoughts heard concurrently.

Mozart continues in great excitement with a magnificent vision of the composer's task:

> I tell you I want to write a finale lasting half an hour! A quartet becoming a quintet becoming a sextet. On and on, wider and wider — all sounds multiplying and rising together — and together making a sound entirely new! . . . I bet you that's how God hears the world. Millions of sounds ascending at once and mixing in His ear to become an unending music, unimaginable to us! . . . That's our job! That's our job, we composers: to combine the inner minds of him and him and him, and her and her — the thoughts of chambermaids and Court Composers — and turn the audience into God.[23]

23. Shaffer, op. cit., p. 527. I am indebted to Dr. Larry Bouchard, of the University of Virginia, for drawing my attention to this passage.

The more facets of a single moment in time that a composer can stage, extending that moment if necessary through prolonged playing time and then connecting it to other similarly attenuated moments, the more he can make the audience hear the world as God does. So, at least, runs Mozart's argument. If he is right, then the theater provides an analogy not only for God's mode of showing himself to men, but also for his mode of simultaneous (and harmonious) perception.

Chapter 3 Imitation and Creation

Thus far, in terms of the theater, we have dealt only with the internal dimensions of a play: how a transformation is effected when text becomes performance, and how the concurrent use of performance time and space creates the distinctively theatrical quality of simultaneous action. We now venture beyond the confines of the play itself to consider the relationship of the imaginative world within the play to the real or imagined world outside it.

A common view of art is that it should provide a recognizable copy of a portion of the real world: the closer the resemblance between art and nature the more skilled the artist. By this criterion, a painting of a horse by Stubbs is preferable to a painting of a horse by Picasso and, on the stage, Laurence Olivier's remarkably "realistic" portrayal of a black Othello is better acting than that of the black actors who wear white masks to represent the European court in Genet's *The Blacks.* Norman Bryson, borrowing a phrase from Husserl, has called this "the natural attitude."[1]

But "the natural attitude" has drawn sophisticated fire. To copy the real world in art, it is objected, is neither possible nor desirable. It is not possible, first, because the artist does not have unmediated access to a world "out there." On the contrary, Bryson maintains, "the reality experienced by human beings is always historically produced."[2] We see,

1. N. Bryson, *Vision and Painting* (London: Macmillan, 1983) pp. 4-5.
2. Ibid., p. 13.

in great part, what our particular time and culture prepare us to see. Heath's rhinoceros, as Gombrich pointed out, owes as much to Dürer as to nature. Secondly, art, like language, is a system of signs. Recent semiotic theory has applied broadly Saussure's observation that, in language, "the bond between the signifier and the signified is arbitrary."[3] That various configurations of paint, for example, should stimulate the same mental concept as the letters "tree" or "arbor" is simply a matter of convention. "Denotation," Nelson Goodman insists, "is the core of representation and is independent of resemblance."[4]

Nor is resemblance, even if it were possible, necessarily desirable. To engage in "the imitative portrayal of phenomena," according to Nietzsche, is to participate in a conspiracy of concealment. Art should be a direct expression of the noumena; theater should be "music made visible." The virtue of Greek tragedy, he believed, was to be "exempt since its beginning from the embarrassing task of copying actuality."[5] In this century, abstract art has celebrated its freedom from that "embarrassing task," and many a literary theorist has followed A. C. Bradley's lead in declaring that the nature of poetry "is to be not a part, nor yet a copy, of the real world (as we commonly understand that phrase), but to be a world by itself, independent, complete, autonomous."[6]

However this may be true of other media, there is in the theater one virtually insurmountable barrier to complete abstraction, one incorrigible link with the world of flesh and blood: the presence of the actor. Though the human body may generate arbitrary sign systems of gesture, movement and expression, the body on stage is not, like the word "corpus" or a particular configuration of paint, an arbitrary signifier of human being. And though Gordon Craig proposed the abolition of the actor, whom he regarded as "an insuperable difficulty"[7]

3. F. de Saussure, *Course in General Linguistics,* trans. W. Baskin (New York: McGraw-Hill, 1959) p. 67.

4. N. Goodman, *Languages of Art* (Indianapolis: Bobbs-Merrill, 1968) p. 5.

5. F. Nietzsche, *The Birth of Tragedy,* trans. F. Golffing (Garden City, New York: Doubleday Anchor, 1956) pp. 105, 89, 50.

6. A. C. Bradley, *Oxford Lectures on Poetry,* 1909 (Bloomington: Indiana University Press, 1961) p. 5.

7. Quoted in J. Roose-Evans, *Experimental Theatre* (New York: Universe Books, 1973) p. 35.

in the way of abstraction, practical experiments in abstract theater, conducted in the early part of this century by the Futurists and the Bauhaus group among others, proved short-lived.[8] The human body, it seems, may be banished from the canvas but not from the stage. Whatever may be true of other art forms, therefore, the theater is irredeemably fleshy, incapable of loosing its link entirely with the world of flesh and blood in which we live.

The theater would appear to exist, therefore, at a point of tension, blessed or handicapped, depending on your point of view, by two limitations: the impossibility of precision copying and the impossibility of pure abstraction. Some may regard the former impossibility as a matter of regret and others the latter. Two theorists generally regarded as being at opposite ends of this spectrum are Aristotle, classical proponent of the doctrine of mimesis, and Antonin Artaud, described by Jacques Derrida as one who above all "wants to have done with the *imitative* concept of art, with the Aristotelian aesthetics."[9] It is not my purpose to attempt precise definition of the nature of theatrical representation and I will deliberately alternate between language borrowed from theories of resemblance, on the one hand, and from semiotic theories, on the other. I do believe, though, that a consideration of Aristotle and Artaud at this point will allow us to stake out some broad common ground from which there may be affirmed, to adapt William Lynch's phrase, a "true and fundamental relevancy of the [theatrical] organism to reality."[10]

Aristotle and Artaud

Aristotle grounds all art in imitation and, at first glance, might appear to be doing so in a highly restrictive fashion, arguing for the closest pos-

8. M. Kirby, *Futurist Performance* (New York: Dutton, 1971) pp. 57-63, 71-119, 278-79, 296-98; O. Schlemmer, L. Moholy-Nagy and F. Molnar, *The Theater of the Bauhaus,* ed. W. Gropius, trans. A. S. Wensingen (Middletown, Conn.: Wesleyan University Press, 1961).

9. J. Derrida, *Writing and Difference,* trans. A. Bass (Chicago: University of Chicago Press, 1978) p. 234.

10. W. F. Lynch, *Christ and Apollo* (Notre Dame: University of Notre Dame Press, 1975) p. x.

sible correspondence between art and nature. Art, he writes, has its origins in an inherent human instinct to imitate and to enjoy works of imitation. "We enjoy looking at the most accurate representations of things which in themselves we find painful to see, such as the forms of the lowest animals and of corpses," because in seeing such "likenesses" we "acquire information," and because there is a fundamental joy of recognition in being able to say, "This is a picture of so and so" (ch. 4).[11] Thus,

> if an artist were to daub his canvas with the most beautiful colours laid on at random, he would not give the same pleasure as he would by drawing a recognizable portrait in black and white. (ch. 6)

In the theater, accordingly, he insists that "characters should be lifelike" (ch. 15).

But a more careful consideration of Aristotle's doctrine of mimesis will belie this initial impression. The very fact that in his opening chapter he is willing to include among the kinds of art that can be "described in general terms as forms of imitation [μίμησις]" not only tragedy and comedy but epic and dithyrambic poetry and "most music composed for the flute and the lyre" (ch. 1) should give us pause. Music is not ordinarily thought of as an art of resemblance and, though Beethoven can have a clarinet imitate the song of a cuckoo in his *Pastoral Symphony,* this is not the kind of "mimetic" music Aristotle had in mind. On the contrary, it would appear that Aristotle envisaged music working in much the same way as dance: "It is by the manner in which [dancers] arrange the rhythms of their movements that they represent men's characters and feelings and actions" (ch. 1). To suggest that the rhythm of a particular sequence of notes or bodily movements conveys or "sounds like" fear or pursuit is to propose a more complex form of imitation than mere copying.

Similarly, when Aristotle discusses tragedy in particular, he lays as much emphasis on the creative as on the imitative work of the artist. This is implicit in his famous definition of tragedy:

> Tragedy . . . is a representation [μίμησις] of an action that is worth serious attention, complete in itself, and of some amplitude; in lan-

11. Aristotle, *On the Art of Poetry,* in *Classical Literary Criticism,* trans. T. S. Dorsch (Harmondsworth: Penguin, 1965) pp. 29-75.

> guage enriched by a variety of artistic devices appropriate to the several parts of the play; presented in the form of action not narration; by means of pity and fear bringing about the purgation of such emotions (ch. 6).

That the language is to be "enriched" rather than copied verbatim from "real life" is tacit admission that the creative artist modifies off-stage "reality." Likewise when Aristotle defines "the representation of the action" as "the plot of the tragedy" and, in that connection, speaks of the poet as "a maker of plots" (ch. 9), "ordering" (ch. 6) and "arranging" the incidents so as to produce a "well-constructed" plot (ch. 7), it is clear that the dramatic poet is not engaged in indiscriminate imitation of history but is drawing selectively from what he believes to be the facts and possibilities of history so as to create something new and "complete in itself." Indeed Aristotle admits that "it is not the poet's function to describe what actually happened, but the kinds of things that might happen." The former is the inferior task of the historian, who is concerned only with "particular facts," while the poet "is concerned with universal truths" (ch. 9). Aristotle's trust in the historian's ability to record "facts" may be problematic for the modern reader, but since the poet is declaratively not an historian, this need not delay us. "The representation [μίμησις] of an action" is the performance of a plot, created by the poet from the raw material of historical possibilities, "lifelike" only in the sense that "it could happen," by means of which universal truths and not historical particularities are presented to the audience. What is more, the purpose of such a performance is not to generate the pleasure of recognizing a likeness ("this is a picture of so and so"), but to generate and purge "pity and fear" with an intensity that life untouched by art cannot match.

According to Aristotle, therefore, performance imitates nature not by aiming at a direct visual and vocal correspondence between the two but, like music and dance, by a kind of indirect resemblance. More importantly, as Aristotle is careful to maintain, a play is not about the "particular facts" that it recalls; it is about "universal truths." The "particular facts" on stage stand in a kind of metaphorical relationship to the "universal truths" that are the drama's ultimate concern. Thus the plot of *Oedipus Rex* imitates, at one level, the tragic downfall of a particular individual who, as the gods predict, unwittingly kills his father and marries his mother. But the plot is also shaped so as to suggest a resemblance between this particular mythic history and a universal truth of human experience. The spectators recognize both that the actor represents Oedipus and that Oedipus represents "someone just like ourselves" (ch. 13). In short, the carefully crafted action on stage recalls, by way of denotation not reproduction, a recognizable narrative which then serves as a partial metaphor for the nature of reality in which the audience lives. The shock of recognition that generates pity and fear is not that "this is a picture of Oedipus" but that "this is a picture of me." Dramatic construct "imitates" history, audience and universal truth.

Whereas, in Aristotle's case, we need to guard against the impression that he is an advocate of slavish imitation, with Artaud the opposite is true: we need to remind ourselves that he is not a proponent of pure abstraction. To be sure, he grieves loudly over the fact that, as he sees it, the theater "is gradually being reduced to a mere inert replica" of "direct, everyday reality" (48);[12] and he argues repeatedly for a form of "poetry in space, . . . created by combinations of lines, shapes, colors, objects in their natural state" and, most especially, by a "pure theatrical language which does without words, a language of signs, gestures and attitudes," "created for" and addressed to "the senses instead of being addressed primarily to the mind as is the language of words" (38-39).

Artaud refuses to copy surfaces, however, not in order to generate pure form but to clear the stage for "another archetypal and dangerous reality." To complete the previous quotation, Artaud longs for a theater that is

> the Double not of this direct, everyday reality of which it is gradually being reduced to a mere inert replica — as empty as it is sugarcoated — but of another archetypal and dangerous reality, a reality of which the Principles, like dolphins, once they have shown their heads, hurry to dive back into the obscurity of the deep. (48)

It is not a question of whether the theater should imitate a reality beyond itself, but of what reality it should imitate. Artaud admits the impossibility of analyzing this other reality philosophically:

12. A. Artaud, *The Theater and Its Double,* trans. M. C. Richards (New York: Grove Press, 1958).

> Only poetically and by seizing upon what is communicative and magnetic in the principles of all the arts can we, by shapes, sounds, music, and volumes, evoke . . . states of an acuteness so intense and so absolute that we sense, beyond the tremors of all music and form, the underlying menace of a chaos as decisive as it is dangerous.

Thus, he claims, we are put in touch with that "essential drama" of which the theater is the double (50-51).

This relationship between the theater and its archetypal double is described by Artaud as one of "magical mimesis" (81). At its most powerful, it is an "excruciating, magical relation to reality and danger" (89) akin to that of

> the old totemism of animals, stones, objects capable of discharging thunderbolts, costumes impregnated with bestial essences – everything, in short, that might determine, disclose, and direct the secret forces of the universe. (10)

Just as "stone comes alive" when shaped into "the Serpent Quetzalcoatl's multiple twists and turns" (10-11), so theatrical signs can also "come alive" and give expression to "sleeping forces."

This is to be done, however, not with words alone – Artaud is vehemently opposed to the notion of theater as "performed text" (68) – but with a language utilizing every aspect of the theater: "music, dance, plastic art, pantomime, mimicry, gesticulation, intonation, architecture, lighting and scenery," a "sign-language," in short "created for the senses" and not just for the intellect (38-39). Sometimes these "signs" will have a natural "ideographic value" (39); at other times they will be "spiritual signs" having "a precise meaning which strikes us only intuitively but with enough violence to make useless any translation into logical discursive language" (54).

Like Aristotle, Artaud drew on the raw material of history and myth. One of his best known scenarios, never translated into performance, was for a *Conquest of Mexico.* This was not to be "realistic": the audience would be surrounded by terrifying "images, movements, dances, rites, . . . fragmented melodies and sudden turns of dialogue" (128), by characters "enlarged to the stature of giant mannikins" (125), multiplied and divided, and by "space . . . stuffed with whirling gestures, horrible faces, dying eyes" (130). But nor was historical reference an embarrassment. The "clash of moral disorder and Catholic monarchy with pagan order" posed not only the historical but also "the alarmingly immediate question of colonization and the right one continent thinks it has to enslave another." Further, it served as a metaphor for the Western loss, as Artaud saw it, of a "pagan" sensibility (126-27), a loss that had impoverished Occidental art in general and the theater in particular. These and the multitude of other particular conflicts to which the scenario refers are intended to stand, both in their historical and theatrical manifestations, as particular instances of that "essential conflict" of which, in the end, Artaud's theater must always be the double.

Aristotle and Artaud are not without their differences, most notably in their attitude to the written text. Aristotle believed that "the effect [of a tragedy] is as vivid when a play is read as when it is acted" (ch. 26), and Artaud railed against "certain theatrical amateurs" for whom "a play read affords just as definite and as great a satisfaction as the same play performed" (117-18). But in matters of imitation and creation they are not as far apart as might at first appear. Is it immediately obvious, for instance, which of the two wrote that "the true purpose of the theater is to create Myths, to express life in its immense, universal aspect, and from that life to extract images in which we find pleasure in discovering ourselves"? The words are Artaud's (116), but they recall Aristotle. Both, if we may now delineate their common ground, view theater as a construct, shaped by the poet or director from the raw materials of historical possibility or myth, claiming neither a precise correspondence to its referent nor an autonomy of pure abstraction, in which the members of the audience recognize signs of an off-stage reality in which they themselves participate. That off-stage reference is threefold: to history or myth, to "universal truth" or "essential drama," and to present audience.

Phèdre in Paris and Iowa

The surprisingly close kinship between Aristotle and Artaud may be illustrated further from two diverse productions of Racine's *Phèdre,* a play shaped in part by a strict, neo-classical reading of Aristotle and in part by a myth as "dangerous" as even Artaud could desire. The play's first production, at the Théâtre de l'Hôtel de Bourgogne in Paris in 1677, took place in a theatrical milieu dominated by a concern for *vraisemblance* ("verisimilitude"); the second production to which I want to draw attention took place at the University of Iowa in 1965 amidst experiments in abstract theater.

When *Phèdre* was first performed, Aristotle's empirical observations were regarded as fixed rules to be applied so that, as Jean Chapelain put it, the audience may be "present at a theatrical action as if at a real action."[13] Even those playwrights who chafed under specific restrictions accepted the basic premise. Corneille wrote:

> The dramatic poem is an imitation, or rather a portrait of human actions, and it is beyond doubt that portraits gain in excellence in proportion as they resemble the original more closely.[14]

It is with some surprise therefore that one moves from theory to practice. Racine's *Phèdre* is no less faithful than its contemporaries to the accepted canons of mimetic verisimilitude. Yet it is far from what we would now call "realistic." The stage directions state only that the action takes place in "Troezen, a town in the Peloponnese," and in all likelihood, the original set represented a single, unspecified space somewhere in town, possibly a courtyard or foyer in the royal palace which, by convention and not architectural realism, led directly to a multitude of neighboring locations. Corneille had suggested that "theatrical place" should represent no one room in particular but "a room contiguous to" all other rooms; T. E. Lawrenson comments that, "in their tussle with the problems of unity of place, the authors have resorted to the drama of entry, the exploitation of place 'whence.'"[15] In other words, in *Phèdre,* the playing area does not represent the apartments of Phèdre, Hippolytus, Theseus and Aricia, nor even the palace entrance, but an abstract space into which each of these open.

13. Quoted in G. Brereton, *French Tragic Drama in the Sixteenth and Seventeenth Centuries* (London: Methuen, 1973) p. 115.

14. Quoted in Adams (ed.), op. cit., p. 223.

15. Corneille, quoted in ibid., p. 226; T. E. Lawrenson, *The French Stage and Playhouse in the XVIIth Century,* 2nd edn (New York: AMS Press, 1986) p. 170.

Nor is the language or the plot what we would call "realistic." Characters from Greek mythology speak in stately alexandrine verse, assigning their passion's cause to gods and goddesses. Royal Phèdre, despite her relentless effort to suppress desire, is consumed with lust for her step-son, Hippolytus, and complains:

> Ce n'est plus une ardeur dans mes veines cachée:
> C'est Vénus tout entière à sa proie attachée. (I, iii)

> [The fire no longer slumbers in the veins.
> Venus in all her might is on her prey.][16]

Hippolytus' death is the extreme case. In the neo-classical theater, deaths and other acts of violence, which, if acted, would appear "unreal," are confined to reported speech. And so we are told that, as Hippolytus fled his father's curse, a sudden storm beached an enormous wave beside his chariot. From its fragments rose a "monstre furieux," so hideous that all but Hippolytus fled in terror. Undaunted, Hippolytus killed the monster but lost control of his terrified horses:

> Ils rougissent le mors d'une sanglante écume.
> On dit qu'on a vu même, en ce désordre affreux,
> Un dieu qui d'aiguillons pressait leur flanc poudreux.
> A travers de rochers la peur les précipite;
> L'essieu crie et se rompt: l'intrépide Hippolyte
> Voit voler en éclats tout son char fracassé;
> Dans les rênes lui-même il tombe embarrassé. (V, vi)

> [They stained the bridle with their bloody foam.
> In this wild tumult, it is even said,
> A god appeared, goading their dusty flanks.
> Over the rocks fear drove them headlong on;
> The axle groaned and broke. Hippolytus
> Saw his whole chariot shattered into bits.
> He fell at last, entangled in the reins.][17]

16. Racine, *Phaedra and Other Plays,* trans. J. Cairncross (Harmondsworth: Penguin, 1963) p. 161.

17. Ibid., p. 211.

While Phèdre's invocation of the goddess of love may reasonably be translated into psychological terms, the account of Hippolytus' death cannot. To explain it away as the overreaction of a highly strung witness to a seaside chariot accident would be laughable. Something much closer to Artaud's "dangerous and archetypal reality" than to "direct, everyday reality" is being evoked.

Verisimilitude, as Tzvetan Todorov points out, is more a question of conformity to genre than it is a matter of direct visual and vocal correspondence to "reality."[18] But *vraisemblance* and relationship to offstage reality are not synonymous. Playing to an aristocratic French audience, obsessed with the need to control passion with reason and natural desire with civilized *vertu* (and, in Racine's view of things, necessarily failing), the action, by way of signs drawn from Greek myth, imitates its audience. George Steiner has suggested that "figuratively,"

> the space of action in the dramas of Racine is that part of Versailles in the immediate vision of the king. Here decorum, containment, self-control, ritual, and total attentiveness are enforced. Even the uttermost of grief or hope must not destroy the cadence of formal speech and gesture.

But such decorum was won at the cost of great and often inhuman *vertu.* Without once transgressing the proprieties of neo-classical decorum, Racine has released "archaic terrors upon a court theatre," terrors not always suppressed beyond "the immediate vision of the king." The formality of the verse is, in Steiner's view, a part of this magic. "By force of incantation" in measured alexandrine, there has been brought "into the seventeenth-century playhouse presences begotten of chaos and ancient night."[19]

One may grope to express the "universal truth" that these "presences" embody and that the play represents in contemporary Jansenist terms, as the absence of grace from one otherwise just,[20] or in modern psychological terms of repressed sexuality and incestuous longing. But, in either case, we can reasonably conclude that the play offered its first

18. T. Todorov, *The Poetics of Prose,* trans. R. Howard (Ithaca, New York: Cornell University Press, 1977) p. 83.

19. G. Steiner, *The Death of Tragedy* (London: Faber & Faber, 1961) pp. 78, 81, 92.

20. A. Arnauld, quoted in Racine, op. cit., p. 133.

audience recognizable dramatic images, shaped from the raw material of myth, that represented, albeit indirectly and in a particularly intense form, facets of the audience's own experience.

Turning to the Iowa production of *Phèdre,* we find a very different theoretical ambience. The director, Lael Woodbury, conceives of theater not in terms of "Aristotle's dictum that tragic drama is the depiction of human action" but as a multi-media creative event,

> a mosaic orchestration of concrete sensory stimuli somewhat parallel to the composer's use of sound, the experimental film maker's light, and dancer's movement, the abstract painter's color, and the architect's space.[21]

Confessedly influenced by Artaud, he pursues a theatricality encompassing but not subservient to narrative recital.

This conception was evident in Woodbury's production of *Phèdre.* He tried, for example, "to explore the sensory aspects of the language," allowing words at times to issue as a bellow or a roar. Costumes were abstract, at most being "intended to suggest" and not to imitate Greek dress, aimed at rendering the characters "handsome" rather than of a particular place and time. The action, "an ideal conflict," free from the accidents of particularity, took place on an octagonal, ornately painted dais, emerging center stage out of the surrounding darkness. Behind this was hung a spider's web of nautical ropes, which the actors would at times lean against or begin to climb. One effect was borrowed from the abstract theater of the Bauhaus. When Theseus was most enraged by his conviction that his wife had betrayed him, a deep, subliminal rumble would issue from beneath the auditorium, "making the whole theatre shake." A throbbing noise, made by a rope attached to a string and whirled around the head, had been recorded, slowed and played back on huge loudspeakers in a cavernous storage room below the auditorium. Woodbury describes it: "You could barely hear it. But you could feel it. It was a quality in the air."[22]

21. L. J. Woodbury, *Mosaic Theatre* (Provo: Brigham Young University Press, 1976) pp. 84, 187.

22. Quoted from a telephone conversation with Mr. Woodbury, 4 June 1987; cf. Woodbury, op. cit., pp. 162, 166. Other material is drawn from Woodbury's unpublished production notes.

All of this, however, was not autonomous theatricality isolated from the world outside performance. On the contrary, it was Woodbury's suggestion that the "commanding metaphor" of Racine's play is that of "sexual confrontation in an arena," and it was this that generated the particular "creative scenic and movement design" of the production.[23] The dais was the arena, the movement pattern circular "around the arena," with Phèdre and Hippolytus constantly confronting one another as if in a duel. Woodbury had initially thought in terms of a bullring, with Phèdre as the matador, Hippolytus as the bull. Not only the arena stage, but words issued as a roar and the sword left in Phèdre's grip, find their place within this concept. The purpose was to "make concrete . . . the spiritual values of Racine's [*Phèdre*]."[24]

The production, in other words, imitated human action and passion, albeit indirectly and in terms of theatrical metaphor. It also imitated its audience. "Sexual confrontation" is not something strange to twentieth-century audiences, and Woodbury's concern, even in his most abstract productions, is that the stage serve "as a mental mirror reflecting a series of symbols, images and impressions evoking half-forgotten sorrows, joys and fears," and asking of the viewer, "Does it tell you more about yourself and your world?"[25]

Whether one invokes, therefore, at a theoretical level, strict mimesis or abstract creativity, seems to make a difference formally but not essentially. In both performances of *Phèdre,* carefully shaped dramatic action, bearing an indirect resemblance to the reality from which its material is drawn, addresses the world in which its audience lives. To use theological terms, word that cannot otherwise be fully expressed becomes in the theater recognizable flesh (and color and sound and movement), shedding light, it is hoped, on the world off stage.

Word, Flesh and Figure

Word becomes flesh; flesh does not illustrate word. Sympathetic to Artaud, Derrida has written scathingly of "the theological stage" as one

23. Woodbury, op. cit., pp. 29-30.
24. Ibid., p. 53.
25. Ibid., p. 175.

which "is dominated by speech, . . . by the layout of a primary logos which does not belong to the theatrical site and governs it from a distance." On such a stage,

> whatever their importance, all the pictorial, musical and even gesticular forms introduced into Western theater can only, in the best of cases, illustrate, accompany, serve, or decorate a text, a verbal fabric, a logos which *is said* in the beginning.[26]

While this may be fair criticism of any tradition in which the theater is regarded as a subdivision of literature, his use of the adjective "theological" to describe such a tradition is open to question. For in the *theatrum gloriae Dei,* if our analysis thus far has been correct, word is not privileged over flesh.

Karl Barth writes that "revelation engenders the Scripture which attests it":

> His Word became flesh of our flesh, blood of our blood. His glory was seen here in the depths of our situation, and the full depths of our situation were disclosed for the first time when he illumined them then and there by the Lord's glory. . . . This happened, and this is what the Old Testament as a word of prophecy and the New Testament as a word of fulfillment both proclaim as having happened, as having happened conclusively, totally and sufficiently.[27]

Artaud envisioned a theater "no longer based on dialogue" prescribed by written text but "created on the stage." This would "culminate . . . in a work *written down,*" but it would be one that had been created not first on the page, but "in nature itself, in real space."[28] This, we might say, is Barth's view of the relationship between Scriptural and homiletic text, on the one hand, and Incarnation, on the other. Textual record was engendered by performance "in nature itself, in real space."

It is striking too that the doctrine of the Incarnation conceives of God as finding the materials in which to express himself in the already existing and recognizable creation. "The Word became flesh" and not

26. Derrida, op. cit., pp. 235-36.
27. Barth, op. cit., 1/1, p. 115.
28. Artaud, op. cit., pp. 111-12.

an unknown substance. Plato had insisted that the final revelation of beauty would not be

> in the likeness of a face or hands or any other part of the bodily frame, or in any form of speech or knowledge, or existing in any individual being, as for example, a living creature, whether in heaven, or in earth, or anywhere else.[29]

The God of Jesus Christ was, it appears, more resourceful, imitating man in order to reveal himself and to invite men to become "imitators [μιμηταί] of God" (Eph. 5:1). The Incarnation, in other words, though it made visible the invisible, entailed the use of recognizable materials and the imitation, "yet without sin" (Heb. 4:15 KJV), of its audience. Creation alone, according to theological formulation, was executed *ex nihilo.*

The rest of salvation history has also been viewed as a divine performance, created "in nature itself, in real space," with signs drawn from the dictionary of nature and human history and denoting "universal" or otherwise "unseen" truth. One thinks, for example, in the Pentateuch, of God's reported use of the rainbow and of circumcision, of the plagues, exodus and sacrificial ordinances. In each of these instances, as the story tells it, prior performance engendered textual interpretation. But it is what Erich Auerbach has called the figural imagination that has most consistently viewed history as an original construct of dramatic signs engendering subsequent textual record.

Auerbach has defined a "figure" as "an occurrence on earth signif[ying] not only itself but at the same time another, which it predicts or confirms, without prejudice to the power of its concrete reality here and now."[30] St. Basil, in the fourth century, described such figures or "types" in mimetic terms, as "a manifestation of things to come through a [present] imitation [μίμησις]."[31] Nor is figural interpretation the invention of "oversubtle" theologians. As V. A. Kolve points out, the Christ of the Gospels "was the first to interpret events as figures," re-

29. Plato, *Symposium,* 211a-b, in *The Dialogues of Plato,* trans. B. Jowett, 4 vols. (Oxford: Clarendon Press, 1953) I, pp. 542-43.

30. E. Auerbach, *Mimesis,* trans. W. R. Trask (Princeton: Princeton University Press, 1953) p. 555.

31. Quoted in Kolve, op. cit., p. 63.

ferring to Moses lifting up the serpent in the desert as a figure of His own crucifixion (Jn 3:14) and to Jonah's three days in the belly of the whale as a figure of His resurrection (Matt. 12:40).[32]

Such figural relationships may also be drawn between events in the seen and unseen worlds. Consider, by way of illustration, the remark of the writer to the Hebrews concerning the exaltation of Christ: "For Christ has entered, not into a sanctuary made with hands, a copy of the true one, but into heaven itself, now to appear in the presence of God on our behalf" (Heb. 9:24). There are at least two mimetic relationships suggested here. First, the tabernacle on earth, the "sanctuary made with hands" in which the Jews worshipped, was "a copy of the true one" in heaven. The author had earlier (8:5) claimed warrant for this idea from the Old Testament text, arguing that the Jews

> serve a copy and a shadow of the heavenly sanctuary; for when Moses was about to erect the tent, he was instructed by God, saying, "See that you make everything according to the pattern that was shown you on the mountain."

Secondly, the annual entry of the Jewish high priest into the Holy of Holies, "taking blood which he offers for himself and for the errors of his people" (9:7) imitates, we are told, the entry "once for all" of Christ "through the greater and more perfect tent" into heaven itself, "taking not the blood of goats and calves but his own blood, thus securing an eternal redemption" (9:11-12). Mimetic links are being suggested not only between the seen and the unseen world but also between past and future: the Holy of Holies on earth "copied" that in heaven and the annual rite of Atonement prefigured the single ascension of Christ to the right hand of God. To use theatrical terms, both the stage setting of the tabernacle on earth and the action of the high priest on that stage denoted an invisible reality in heaven.

Such mimetic links between seen and unseen worlds, between present worship and archetypal history, continue under the new covenant. For, according to the writer to the Hebrews, the ascension of Christ gained for each New Testament believer the freedom to imitate Christ's entry into heaven. "We have confidence," the writer affirms,

32. Ibid., p. 64.

"to enter the sanctuary by the blood of Jesus" (10:19). Philip Hughes comments, "It is no earthly sanctuary into which the Christian believer is invited to enter, for the Mosaic structure was but an insubstantial shadow of the heavenly reality." Rather, the Christian is granted "freedom of access" into "the true sanctuary" of heaven itself.[33] That this access is a present enjoyment of the worshipping Christian was insisted on by the Puritan scholar John Owen: "They are . . . mistaken who suppose the entrance into the most holy to be an entrance into heaven after this life." For the contrast being drawn is between constraints under the old covenant and freedom of worship under the new. To "enter the sanctuary," according to Owen, "doth consist in our drawing nigh unto God in holy services and worship through Christ."[34] Under the New Testament, therefore, the heavenly tabernacle continues to have its "copy" on earth, no longer a building "made with hands" but now one fashioned by the Spirit. The Letter to the Ephesians speaks of Jew and Gentile being "joined together . . . into a holy temple in the Lord, . . . a dwelling place of God in the Spirit" (2:21-22). To use theatrical terms again, the members of the New Testament audience are invited to participate in the drama, imitating in their corporate life and in their worship, "both public and private,"[35] the "true" heavenly temple and the pioneer entry of Christ into heaven on their behalf.

The Slaughter of the Innocents

The figural view that heaven and earth, past, present and future, form a unified complex of mimetic relationships found its most concise theatrical expression in the liturgical drama of the medieval Church. One of the more intricately crafted of these plays is the Fleury *Slaughter of the Innocents,* dating from the twelfth century. A consideration of its text and probable performance will provide us with an example not only of a play growing directly out of the Church's understanding of biblical typology but also of the immensely creative way in which the imitation

33. P. E. Hughes, *A Commentary on the Epistle to the Hebrews* (Grand Rapids: Eerdmans, 1977) pp. 406-7.

34. J. Owen, *An Exposition of the Epistle to the Hebrews,* 1668-84, ed. W. H. Goold, 7 vols. (Edinburgh: Johnstone and Hunter, 1885) VI, p. 501.

35. Ibid., p. 509.

of natural and historical phenomena, on the one hand, and of action in the unseen world, on the other, may be forged into a unified theatrical whole.

The Slaughter of the Innocents was performed annually, probably after matins on 28 December (the Feast of the Innocents) in the monastery church of St. Benoît-sur-Loire; the actors were the monks and choirboys of the monastery. The play opens with several of the younger choirboys, dressed in white stoles, parading informally through the church, rejoicing and singing the antiphon of vespers for the Vigil of All Saints:

> O how glorious is the kingdom in which with Christ all the sanctified ones sing praises, clad in white stoles; they follow the lamb whithersoever he may go.[36]

Immediately, with this deceptively simple beginning, a threefold time frame has been established. Ostensibly the boys represent the Jewish children, shortly to be murdered by Herod's soldiers on the presumption that one of them is the Christ child (Matt. 2:16). But, by their costume and choice of antiphon, they also represent the virgin martyrs of all ages, "slain for the word of God and for the witness they had borne . . . , each given a white robe" (Rev. 6:9, 11) and identified with those "who have not defiled themselves with women," but "who follow the Lamb wherever he goes" (Rev. 14:4). The choirboys also represent themselves and the other members of the monastic community. The monastery church, with its constant round of worship, is a type of the heavenly kingdom, "in which with Christ all the sanctified ones sing praises." The white stoles are priestly garments, worn by the celebrant in the Mass. And, like the Innocents slain by Herod and the martyrs of the book of Revelation, the monks and choirboys are devoted to chastity. At least three different groups of people, therefore, from three distinct historical time periods, are being "imitated" by a single procession of choirboys.

This multiple and simultaneous temporal mimesis is sustained throughout. A lamb representing Christ, perhaps played by a boy draped in a real sheepskin, joins the procession of choirboys, Innocents

36. *The Slaughter of the Innocents,* trans. D. Bevington, in D. Bevington (ed.), *Medieval Drama* (Boston: Houghton Mifflin, 1975) pp. 67-72.

and martyrs, and leads them eastward through the church towards the choir stalls. At the same time monks playing Joseph and Mary take a baby, who is also Christ, the archetypical Innocent and martyr, to safety in Egypt at the west door of the church; and Herod, enraged by the rumors of a rival King of the Jews, orders that the boys be killed. The choirboys sing:

> To the hallowed lamb slain for us,
> To Christ, we consecrate, under this banner of light,
> The splendor of the Father, the splendor of virginity.[37]

The words are appropriate to all three of their roles: Innocents, martyrs and aspirant monks.

The ceremonially enacted slaughter is followed by a meditative interlude in which Rachel mourns their death. Here the mimetic relationship with "real" time becomes even more complex, for Rachel's outpouring of grief imitates at least six distinct historical actions. First and most obviously she represents the Jewish mothers weeping for their slaughtered children (Matt. 2:16-18). The evangelist had named this group of anonymous women Rachel by way of reference to Jeremiah's description, six centuries earlier, of Jewish mothers mourning the departure of their children for Babylon from the deportation center of Ramah:

> A voice was heard in Ramah,
> wailing and loud lamentation,
> Rachel weeping for her children;
> she refused to be consoled,
> because they were no more. (Matt. 2:18; Jer. 31:15)

Jeremiah in turn had collectively named these women Rachel after the Hebrew matriarch buried near Ramah (1 Sam. 10:2). Just as Israel designates all the descendants of the patriarch so the name of his wife designates their female descendants. "Rachel weeping for her children" at Fleury therefore denotes not only the Jewish mothers lamenting the

37. Bevington translates "virginitatis" here as "the virgin birth." V. A. Kolve has suggested to me that "virginitatis" refers in this instance not to the virginity of Mary but to that of the boys and those whom they represent.

murder of their children by Herod's soldiers, but the earlier mothers bewailing the exile of their sons, Rachel herself grieving as if from the grave over the sufferings of her people and, by implication, Mary's confusion and sorrow over the exile of the Christ child to Egypt. But this is not just a Jewish grief. Just as Israel can designate the patriarch's spiritual as well as physical heirs (Gal. 6:16), so can Rachel. Here she represents the Church, the Mother of God's people, saddened by the loss of all her martyred sons. Finally, Rachel sings, "My soul is troubled within me," the antiphon of lauds for Good Friday associated indelibly with the Mater Dolorosa. The monastic actor is therefore also consciously recalling the Virgin Mary weeping over her own son's death on the cross.

It is a remarkable moment: a single actor's simulated grief imitates the mourning of the Virgin Mary on the flight to Egypt and at the foot of the cross, the mothers of the Innocents and of the exiles, suffering Israel and the persecuted Church. The choirboys lying on the chancel steps recall Christ crucified, the slaughtered Innocents and martyrs, Jewish exiles and the monastic community itself, exiled from the world.

Their grief is not, however, without consolation. As in Jeremiah's account Rachel was told:

> Keep your voice from weeping,
> and your eyes from tears;
> for your work shall be rewarded, says the LORD,
> and [your children] shall come back from the land
> of the enemy, (Jer. 31:16)

so at Fleury Rachel is comforted, in all her roles, with the promise that her sons now "live blessed above the stars." As the Jewish exiles were promised eventual return to their homeland, so the faithful martyrs of all ages are assured a blessed inheritance in heaven. While Herod dies, therefore, and his corpse is "removed," to be replaced by his son Archelaus, the Innocents/martyrs/choirboys are, like Christ, raised from the dead; an angel, high in the church, perhaps on top of the rood screen, sings to them the words of Jesus: "Suffer the little ones to come unto me, for of such is the kingdom of heaven" (Matt. 19:14). Joseph and Mary return rejoicing from exile in Egypt, and the entire cast and congregation join in singing the *Te Deum.*

The anonymous Fleury playwright created a brief dramatic image, within the confines of a monastery church and a liturgical setting, that is brimming with polysemic mimetic references across time and space and throughout the seen and unseen world. Yet he has crafted them into a unified artistic whole in which each reference interacts with and enriches all the others.

Now, I am well aware that nearly two decades ago Nathan Scott pronounced the death, "not so much of God as of the capacity, in the people of our age, for any kind of figural thought." Nor was Scott in any "hurry to lament the passing of figuralism," sensing that "it very much needed to die, if any real access to full maturity were to be won." The figural imagination, for him, has a tendency to reduce the world in which we live to a "mere shadow of the Eternal."[38] For myself, I am not so sure. Auerbach, after all, in the definition cited earlier, is at pains to insist that a historical sign may have an unseen referent "without any prejudice to the power of its concrete reality here and now." And that the people of the last two decades have shown a remarkable revival of interest, to use Peter Berger's phrase, in "rumours of angels"[39] suggests a resilient capacity for all kinds of supernatural thought.

But it is not my purpose to argue here for the potential of the figural imagination to produce, in Scott's words, "a cogent rendering of experience."[40] My far more modest proposal at this point is that the figural scheme of things can provide an apt analogy for theatrical art. As God, it is claimed, shapes from the raw material of nature and human history sensible images that express otherwise inaccessible truth about the world in which his people live, so the playwright or director shapes from the same raw material, viewed through the lens of tradition, sensible dramatic images of "universal truth" about the "world" in which his or her audience lives. *The Slaughter of the Innocents* signifies both sides of the analogy: the monastic community created from traditional material dramatic images of God's theatrical and figural design wrought in human history.

We are reminded once more of the theatricality of the Christian

38. N. A. Scott, Jr., *The Wild Prayer of Longing* (New Haven, Conn.: Yale University Press, 1971) pp. 22-23 and xv.

39. P. L. Berger, *A Rumor of Angels* (Garden City, New York: Doubleday, 1970).

40. Scott, op. cit., p. 23.

tradition. Though Christianity is in one sense a religion of the Book, relying heavily on written testimony, it is in another and arguably primary sense a religion of the Stage. The book claims to record and interpret performance. Whether that performance is thick with signs, as the figural imagination suggests, or more simply centered on the identity of Word and flesh in Jesus of Nazareth, faith is shaped first not by distant text but by performance in the medium and in the midst of human flesh and blood.

Chapter 4 Performance and Audience

Although text may exist without a reader, it is hard to imagine theatrical performance surviving long without an audience. In the last chapter, we spoke of the way in which performance denotes or imitates, among other things, the world of its audience. We now turn our attention to a second aspect of this relationship between stage and auditorium, namely the effect of performance on audience and, contrariwise, of audience on performance.

At the same time, we can pursue further another idea alluded to earlier. Joachim Jeremias has written that Jesus' parables are not primarily "literary productions," having as their object "to lay down general maxims." On the contrary, "each of them was uttered in an actual situation of the life of Jesus," and "every one of them calls for immediate response" on the part of those to whom they were spoken or before whom they were acted. "Jesus spoke to men of flesh and blood; he addressed himself to the situation of the moment," and among the questions that must be asked if we are to "hear again [the] authentic voice" of Jesus of Nazareth is this: "What must have been the effect of his word [and act] upon his hearers?"[1] We must ask, in other words, concerning the relationship between Jesus and his audience.

So potent can this relationship between actor and audience become that it can generate suppression by those responsible for maintaining "order." The Sanhedrin conspired to have Jesus put to death for

1. Jeremias, op. cit., pp. 21-22.

fear that "this man [who] performs many signs" would so influence the crowds as to bring political instability (Jn. 11:48). Civil and ecclesiastical authorities have, over the centuries, made many an effort to intervene in the relationship between stage and auditorium, at times going so far as to close the theaters altogether. This too will form part of our discussion of performance and audience. Finally, however, I will suggest that, though it is a legitimate function of the theater at times to generate fear and anger, play may also be "a source of mirth and gladness."[2]

Theater and the Affective Fallacy

Some literary critics have tended to isolate the play from its audience as a matter of principle. W. K. Wimsatt and Monroe Beardsley, in one of the more influential modern essays in literary theory, coined the term "the affective fallacy" for what they saw as "a confusion between the poem and its *results* (what it *is* and what it *does*)." Any approach, they wrote, which tries "to derive the standard of criticism from the psychological effects of the poem" is to be avoided, for its "outcome . . . is that the poem itself, as an object of specifically critical judgment, tends to disappear." As an "early example of affective theory," they cited Aristotle's theory of "catharsis."[3]

While such an admonition may be of value to students of poetry, it is best set aside when one enters the theater. For dramatic text is not a "poem" but a score for performance in which the audience play an integral part. Consider, by way of lively illustration, the last Dada *soirée* in Zurich, in 1919, directed by Tristan Tzara and attended by an audience expecting to take offense at the Dadaists' anarchist politics and avantegarde art. A speech on abstract art, a dancer wearing a Cubist-style African mask, and some free-association poems began the evening. The latter drew laughter and a few catcalls. Then, in the words of Hans Richter, "all hell broke loose." The 20 Dadaists on stage began speaking, singing, whistling, crowing, sighing, stuttering and yodelling, simultaneously and not always in time, the 20 texts that together formed a

2. Kolve, op. cit., p. 131.

3. W. K. Wimsatt and M. C. Beardsley, *The Verbal Icon* (Lexington: University of Kentucky Press, 1954), pp. 21, 28.

poème simultané. The audience responded with "shouts, whistles, chanting in unison, laughter . . . , all of which mingled more or less anti-harmoniously with the bellowing of the twenty on the platform." Order was temporarily restored by a convenient interval.

The program resumed with an actor cursing both audience and performers, with "anti-tunes" and with dances set to the atonal music of Schoenberg. Then Walter Serner, dressed immaculately as if for a wedding, offered a bouquet of artificial flowers to a headless tailor's dummy to smell and, sitting astride a chair with his back to the audience, began to read from his own anarchistic credo, "Final Dissolution." "The tension in the hall became unbearable. At first it was so quiet you could have heard a pin drop." Soon tense silence gave way to catcalls and then to angry invective. Finally, members of the audience "leaped on to the stage," brandishing pieces of the centuries-old gallery balustrade, "chased Serner into the wings and out of the building, smashed the tailor's dummy and the chair, and stamped on the bouquet." Hans Richter remembers, in the ensuing uproar, a newspaper reporter grasping him by the tie and shouting "ten times over, without pausing for breath, 'You're a sensible man normally.'" The performance was stopped, the auditorium lights turned on, and "faces distorted by rage gradually returned to normal." Richter comments:

> People were realizing that not only Serner's provocations, but also the rage of those provoked, had something inhuman . . . and that this had been the reason for Serner's performance in the first place.

After a 20-minute interval, the show resumed. The final third included a ballet, in which the "pretty faces" and "slender figures" of the dancers were hidden behind "savage Negro masks" and "abstract costumes," poems by Serner, and some anti-music "which left no tone unturned." All was allowed to pass without incident, and this too was part of the intended effect. Richter boasts:

> Tzara had organized the whole thing with the magnificent precision of a ring-master marshalling his menagerie of lions, elephants, snakes and crocodiles. . . . the public was tamed.[4]

4. H. Richter, *Dada: Art and Anti-art* (New York: Harry N. Abrams, 1965) pp. 77-80.

To isolate the performance, in this instance, from its effect on the audience, would mean that the theatrical event itself, "as an object of specifically critical judgment," would "disappear"!

Épatant les bourgeois is not the only option open to a company of actors. Aristotle, if we accept the traditional translation, described Greek tragedy as "through pity and fear effecting the purgation of these emotions" (ch. 6).[5] Dryden, echoing Horace, proposed that a play should have as its purpose, "the delight and instruction" of its audience.[6] Nietzsche declared that "enchantment is the precondition of all dramatic art," and that, in Greek tragedy, it was the role of the chorus "so to excite the mood of the listeners that when the tragic hero appeared they would behold not the awkwardly masked man but a figure borne of their own rapt vision."[7] Marinetti wanted the audience to join "noisily in the action, in the singing, accompanying the orchestra, communicating with the actors in surprising actions and bizarre dialogues."[8]

Artaud, in 1926, announced the search for an audience willing to "join forces" with him in a theatrical experiment whose effect he described, in a sense peculiarly his own, as "cruel," at once painful and therapeutic. The spectator, Artaud wrote, must approach the theater as he might a surgeon,

> knowing, of course, that he will not die, but that it is a serious thing and he will not come out of it unscathed. . . . He must be totally convinced that we are capable of making him scream.[9]

For theater is like the plague. Human perversity reaches a point where it demands expression. The plague meets this need, releasing and finally exhausting the dark forces so that, after the necessary delirium, peace returns. To the degree that theater stimulates and expresses, in an interval of deadly serious but nonetheless controlled play, the "la-

5. S. H. Butcher, *Aristotle's Theory of Poetry and Fine Art,* 4th edn, 1911 (New York: Dover, 1951) p. 23.

6. J. Dryden, "An Essay of Dramatick Poesie," 1668, in B. H. Clark (ed.), *European Theories of the Drama* (New York: Crown, 1947) p. 176.

7. Nietzsche, op. cit., pp. 56, 58.

8. F. T. Marinetti, "The Variety Theatre," in Kirby, op. cit., p. 181.

9. A. Artaud, *Selected Writings,* ed. S. Sontag, trans. H. Weaver (New York: Farrar, Strauss and Giroux, 1976) pp. 155-57.

tent cruelty" of an audience, to that degree, Artaud believed, it preempts the uncontrolled expression of such cruelty outside the theater and is therefore therapeutic.[10]

Brecht took a different stance, arguing that "whatever is intended to produce hypnosis, is likely to induce sordid intoxication, or creates fog," is tantamount to "witchcraft" and "has got to be given up." He advocated a theater in which "the spectator, instead of being enabled to have an experience, is forced as it were to cast his vote."[11] Theatrical *Verfremdungseffekt* was sought as a means to this end. In the hope that unexpected inversion might enable his audience to see familiar evils in a fresh light, he gave the "respectable" goals of a capitalist businessman to the gangster Macheath, and the trading acumen of the capitalist merchant to the vagrant camp-follower Mother Courage. Songs, placards and narrators interrupted the action, reminding the audience that it was watching a play and that a critical attitude was required. It is not that Brecht was opposed to arousing emotion; but emotion should stem from a discriminating response to the action on stage. Anger at Mother Courage's determination to profit at all costs from the war that kills her children is an appropriate response; admiration for her "courageous" decision to press on regardless is not.

From Aristotle to Brecht, it has been the consistent refrain of those who work in or with the theater that the effect of performance on audience is an integral part of the theatrical whole. Francisque Sarcey, the great nineteenth-century French theater critic, stated bluntly, "We cannot conceive of a play without an audience." Stage, lighting, scenery and costume may be dispensed with, "but a play without an audience is inconceivable."[12]

Nor is the relationship between stage and auditorium influential in one direction only. Sarcey notes the effect of "different ways of seeing" on stage conventions. "When the eyes of the audience change," techniques designed to create "the illusion of life" on stage must also change. What is deemed realistic in one epoch will be artificial in another.[13] And Peter Brook has noted the effect of different audiences on

10. Artaud, *The Theater and Its Double,* p. 24.

11. *Brecht on Theatre,* trans. J. Willett (New York: Hill & Wang, 1964) pp. 38-39.

12. F. Sarcey, "Essai d'une esthétique de théâtre," 1876, in Clark (ed.), op. cit., p. 391.

13. Sarcey, op. cit., p. 393.

a single production. In 1964 the Royal Shakespeare Company took Brook's production of *King Lear* to Eastern Europe. "The best performances," Brook recalls, "lay between Budapest and Moscow":

> It was fascinating to see how an audience composed largely of people with little knowledge of English could so influence a cast. These audiences brought with them three things: a love for the play itself, real hunger for a contact with foreigners and, above all, an experience of life in Europe in the last years that enabled them to come directly to the play's painful themes. The quality of the attention that this audience brought expressed itself in silence and concentration; a feeling in the house that affected the actors as though a brilliant light were turned on their work. As a result, the most obscure passages were illuminated; they were played with a complexity of meaning and a fine use of the English language that few of the audience could literally follow, but which all could sense.

When the tour reached the United States, however, the audience was different, made up of people who came "for all the conventional reasons – because it was a social event, because their wives insisted, and so on." The austerity of the production, "which had seemed so right in Europe," bored this audience, and the actors responded by emphasizing action and melodrama, playing "louder and cruder," speeding through the intricate passages that had shone so brightly in Europe. Though text remained constant, the performance had changed and not for the better. Brook realized that "to involve this particular audience in *King Lear*" and to do so "without condescension" would have meant starting again from scratch, building an entirely different production and hence yet another series of performances.[14]

No doubt too the response to *King Lear* of the Eastern European audience was very different from that of its original Jacobean counterpart. The relationship between performance and audience has to be conceived not in terms of a constant text and a transhistorical audience, but in terms of a series of relationships between particular performances and local, historically embedded audiences. This is just the point that Jeremias was making concerning the spoken parables and "parabolic actions" of Jesus.

14. P. Brook, *The Empty Space* (New York: Avon/Discus, 1968) pp. 20-21.

Jesus and His Audiences

Épater les Pharisiens, to dumbfound the Pharisees, seems to have been Jesus' motive on a number of occasions. One thinks, for example, of his public violation of the conventional Sabbath. In Luke's account of the healing of the man "whose right hand was withered" (6:6-11), Jesus went out of his way to secure an audience for his action. Rather than wait for an opportunity to heal unobserved, he summoned the disabled man from his seat in the crowd to center stage: "Come and stand here." "Here" is where "the scribes and the Pharisees watched [Jesus], to see whether he would heal on the Sabbath." Then he addressed the Pharisees directly, engaging their undivided attention and letting them know that he was fully aware both of being watched and of the issues at stake: "I ask you, is it lawful on the sabbath to do good or to do harm, to save life or to destroy it?" His audience remained silent and, like any good actor, Jesus prolonged the moment of tension as long as possible. Slowly turning to gaze on every portion of his audience, we are told, "he looked around on them all." Only then did he say to the man, "Stretch out your hand." The Pharisees "were filled with fury."

One thinks too of the account of Jesus' provocation of the Pharisees at the feast of Tabernacles (Jn. 7:1ff.). Arriving in Jerusalem incognito (7:10), it was not until "about the middle of the feast" (7:14) that Jesus drew attention to himself by teaching in the temple. Then, "on the last day of the feast" (7:37), while the temple guards were under orders to arrest him (7:32), he intensified his incitement of the Jewish leaders. One of the notable features of the feast was that a priest would daily draw water in a golden flagon from the pool of Siloam and carry it in procession to the temple, where, to the accompaniment of Levitical trumpets and popular hallelujahs, it would be poured on the base of the altar. This ritual of water was by way of thanksgiving for rain, for the miraculous supply of water from the rock in the wilderness, and in anticipation of the promised outpouring of the Holy Spirit. Against this background, Jesus "stood up," placing himself, as Leon Morris observes, "in a position to make the maximum number of people see and hear him," and "proclaimed" to the crowd that he was the fulfillment of ritual and type, the true Rock, whose striking would bring the outpouring of the Holy Spirit

(7:37).[15] So affected were the temple guards that they failed to arrest him, reporting back to the Pharisees, "No man ever spoke like this man!" (7:43).

An overnight interval and an attempt by the Pharisees to script and stage the next day's action may have followed (7:53–8:11). Certainly the text tells of direct public confrontation with the Pharisees. Taking his cue from another prominent feature of the feast, the lighting of the temple candelabra in commemoration of the guidance of the Pillar of Fire in the wilderness, Jesus declared himself to be the "light of the world" (8:12).[16] The Pharisees, taking offense, became increasingly belligerent and Jesus responded by pronouncing them neither children of Abraham nor of God but of the devil (8:39-44) and himself the I AM who was even before Abraham (8:58). The Pharisees, enraged, "took up stones to throw at him," but Jesus "hid himself, and went out of the temple" (8:59).

One is reminded, in the pattern of alternating provocation and withdrawal, of Tzara's precise orchestration of audience response in Zurich. Tzara's goal was to force his audience to face the discrepancy between its bourgeois claims to good order and its inherent propensity for destructive rage. Jesus' purpose too seems to have been, in part, to bring to light what he saw as a dissonance between Jewish claims to piety and obedience to the law, on the one hand, and their hardness of heart towards God on the other. Those who would stone the Christ, the fulfillment of Old Testament type, ceremony and promise, were not, as they believed, spiritual "children of Abraham."

Not all that Jesus said and did should be thought of in terms of Dada tactics of provocation. Other "enacted parables" seem to have aimed instead at a kind of Brechtian *Verfremdungseffekt.* Where Brecht gave gangsters and camp followers the manners and motives of capitalists, hoping to jolt his audience into seeing capitalists in a different light, Jesus cast himself in the role of servant, hoping that his disciples might be shocked into seeing their own potential role as leaders in a fresh light. During his final Passover meal with his disciples, Jesus rose

15. L. Morris, *The Gospel According to John* (Grand Rapids: Eerdmans, 1971) pp. 420-22; Dods, op. cit., pp. 245-46; F. L. Godet, *Commentary on John's Gospel,* 1886 (Grand Rapids: Kregel, 1978) pp. 634-36.

16. Dods, op. cit., pp. 273-74.

from the communal table, "laid aside his garments, and girded himself with a towel" (Jn. 13:4). Costumed now as a servant, and using the stage properties of basin and water provided by the owner of the house, Jesus began without a word to wash his disciples' feet. Peter broke the silence first. That Jesus should play the part of the most menial domestic servant was deeply unnerving to him. Jesus promised that Peter would understand later and insisted that the action was necessary if Peter were to take his part with Christ in the ongoing narrative (Ἐὰν μὴ νίψω σε, οὐκ ἔχεις μέρος μετ' ἐμοῦ [13:8]). Only when Jesus had completed his "act without words," doffed his costume, dressed again in his own clothes and resumed his place at the table, did he offer an explanation of his performance. It had been a "example" for their imitation: after his death they were not to engage in a struggle for power but to lead by serving one another.

The crucifixion no doubt produced an even greater *Verfremdungseffekt.* That the promised Messiah and King of the Jews should further descend the social scale, passing from the role of servant to that of condemned criminal, dying, not in "play" but in reality, before a large and hostile audience, at the hands of the Roman authorities, at first completely disoriented the disciples. To the world at large, it remained so alienating as to be, Paul reports, "a stumbling block to Jews and folly to Gentiles" (1 Cor. 1:23). But, according to the New Testament witness, the crucifixion had been scripted from the beginning (Acts 2:23) and, in a dazzling inversion of human expectation, displayed "to those who [were] called . . . , Christ the power of God and the wisdom of God" (1 Cor. 1:24-25).

It is not my purpose to suggest that Brecht and the Dadaists provide the only theatrical paradigms by which to conceive of Jesus' relationship to his audiences. But, if Jeremias is correct and the greater part of the parables, spoken and enacted, "are weapons of warfare," calling for "immediate response,"[17] then these are more likely paradigms than, for example, the more genteel Horatian vision of a theater that delights and instructs. There are other avenues that one could pursue, however. The events of Passion Week could be thought of in terms of Artaud's Theater of Cruelty: a release of the worst in men became, in the retrospect of Christian faith, a means of reconciliation and

17. Jeremias, op. cit., p. 21.

healing. One could think too, remembering Peter Brook's description of touring with *King Lear*, of the effect of particular audiences on Jesus' "performance." In "his own country," we are told, "he could do no mighty work . . . , because of their unbelief" (Mark 6:1-6).

Anti-theatrical Prejudice

But it is time now to return to the theater and to consider the fear generated by its potential for powerful and immediate effect on an audience. For it is not only the literary critic and the Pharisee who have wanted to isolate the theatrical artifact from its audience. At several points in cultural history, guardians of the public morals, whether political or ecclesiastic, have borne testimony to the affective power of the theater by attempting to suppress it.

Before we deal directly with what Jonas Barish has called "the anti-theatrical prejudice," it is worth mentioning certain features of theatrical performance that render it more immediately potent than a purely literary medium. There is, first, the simultaneity of stimuli in the theater. As we observed previously, a reader receives impressions one at a time, an audience from several sources at once. This makes possible a sensory bombardment of an audience more intense than anything the printed word alone can accomplish. Artaud's vision of a performance that would "physically envelop the spectator and immerse him in a constant bath of light, images, movements and noises"[18] is a theatrical and not a literary vision. There is, in addition, the immediacy of response required in the theater. While a reader can lift his eyes from the page to meditate on what he has read, an audience cannot pause in the same way during a performance. Rumination must follow, it cannot accompany performance. Finally, there is the singularity of the audience. It is no accident of grammar that audience is a singular noun. Whereas a multiplicity of readers interact with one another only through the medium of opinion expressed, in conversation or in printed criticism, before or after reading, the members of a theater audience influence one another, and therefore influence one another's reactions and, if Peter Brook is correct, the ongoing performance itself, during performance. An audience tends to re-

18. Artaud, *The Theater and Its Double*, p. 125.

spond as a unit. Excitement generates excitement, yawning is contagious. The theater therefore can affect spectators not just one at a time, as a text must influence its readers, but *en masse,* as an orator can affect a crowd.

All of this has bred fear in those who want to control the ways in which a public is affected. Plato is the first in whom we find what Barish calls "a characteristic conflict: a haunting acknowledgment of the potency of the theater leading to an all the more stinging repudiation of it."[19] The problem with the theater, according to Plato, is that it imitates reprehensible passions and thereby "feeds and waters"[20] such passions in its audience. Aristotle's contention that tragedy purges its audiences of pity and fear may well have been offered by way of defense against this view.

Interestingly it was the development of the theater from staid recitation to a fully sensory medium that, for Plato, constituted its downfall. So long as "theater" consisted of a single "poet" reciting approved prayers and paeans to the gods before an audience policed by "directors of public instruction," all was well. But when poets, in order to please their listeners, started to introduce "vulgar and lawless innovation," experimenting with mixtures of genres and new instrumental timbres, then before long "an evil sort of theatrocracy" grew up, exerting powerful and deplorable influence on the public.[21] It was the distinctively sensory nature of the theater when compared to the written word that warranted Plato's untroubled use of written dialogue to condemn dialogue performed. The former aroused the passions; the latter more readily yielded, in Martha Nussbaum's phrase, "a dry and abstract tone" conducive to clear thinking.[22]

The early Church, influenced both by its neo-Platonic distrust of "passions" and of sensory pleasure and by the decadence of the Roman theater, in which the borderline between play and reality was crossed whenever, for example, an "actor" was torn apart by lions in fact and not pretence, echoed Plato's condemnation of the theater. Tertullian, not unjustly, given the historical circumstances, accused the theater of

19. Barish, op. cit., p. 5.

20. Plato, *The Republic,* X, 606d, in Jowett, trans., op. cit., II, p. 482.

21. Plato, *The Laws,* III, 700a-701b, in Jowett, trans., op. cit., IV, pp. 269-70; Barish, op. cit., pp. 26-28.

22. M. Nussbaum, *The Fragility of Goodness* (Cambridge: Cambridge University Press, 1986) p. 131.

deliberately provoking its audiences to frenzy.[23] Augustine, as Artaud pointed out, was the first to compare the theater to the plague. It was ironic, Augustine argued, that the Roman authorities should, in time of plague, try to appease the gods by commanding plays,

> for the strategy of the evil Spirits, foreseeing that the contagion would end with the body, seized joyfully upon this occasion to introduce a much more dangerous scourge among you, one that attacks not bodies but customs.

Paraphrasing Augustine, Artaud wrote that the theater is, like the plague, a "contagious delirium."[24] Artaud approved. Augustine, following Plato, did not.

The Protestant Reformers and especially their Puritan successors were the most strident heirs of the Church Fathers in this respect, rehearsing all the old bromides about the immoral influence of the theater. Particularly prominent in their argument was the accusation that players are hypocrites. Had not Jesus charged the Pharisees with hypocrisy and did not the word mean "play-acting"? What, demands William Prynne, is hypocrisy

> in the proper signification of the word, but the acting of another's part or person on the stage; or what else is an hypocrite, in his true etymology, but a stage-player, or one who acts another's part, as sundry authors and grammarians teach us?[25]

But the argument from Jesus' repudiation of the Pharisees can work the other way. It may suggest that, while Jesus is alert to the potential for theatrical action in public life, he condemns it only when it implies, in Ulrich Wilckens' phrase, a "jarring contradiction between . . . the outward appearance and the inward lack of righteousness."[26] Such is not

23. Barish, op. cit., p. 45.

24. Augustine, *The City of God,* I, 32, cited in Artaud, *The Theater and Its Double,* p. 26.

25. W. Prynne, *Historiomastix* (London, 1633), quoted in Barish, op. cit., p. 91. I have modernized spelling and punctuation.

26. U. Wilckens, "ὑποκρίνομαι . . . . ," *Theological Dictionary of the New Testament,* eds. G. Kittel and G. Friedrich, trans. G. W. Bromiley, 10 vols. (Grand Rapids: Eerdmans, 1964-76) VIII, p. 559.

the case in Jesus' own "play-acting." Nor is it the case with an actor who makes no pretence of being, in his private life, the hero or, for that matter, the villain he plays on stage. It is not therefore "playing" that Jesus condemns but the dissonance between public facade and private sin.

There are other reasons, besides those inherited from the Church Fathers, why the Reformers may have been suspicious of the theater. Many of them received their early training as humanist scholars and would have been sympathetic to the nascent neo-classicism so foreign to the popular drama of the time with its unabashed mixture of sanctity and scurrility. Others found offensive the presence, in the Corpus Christi plays and their kin, of Roman Catholic doctrines. The very fact that the cycle plays were attached to the Corpus Christi feast, with its celebration of the controversial doctrine of transubstantiation, probably doomed the plays in England.

But Michael O'Connell has argued for the presence of a repugnance to the theater even more basic than any of these. According to O'Connell, the Puritans were persuaded, like Plato, that theater "overpowers by the fulness of its sensual appeal. One is surrounded by the visual sumptuousness of the playhouse itself, by the motion and gesture of the actors' bodies, and by the aural richness of poetic speech."[27] There is a connection, he believes, between the Puritan distrust of the theater and the Protestant Reformers' insistence on the exclusive authority of the written word. Not only do both entail a reaction against the predominantly oral and "incarnational" culture of the Middle Ages, but both also seem to forget that God spoke in Christ a sensual Word. Philip Stubbes, an early Puritan opponent of the theater quoted by O'Connell, maintained that, in the Gospel of John, "we are taught that the word is God, and God is the word," and that "whosoever abuseth the majesty of God in the same" by amending or adding to the biblical narrative on stage "purchaseth to himself eternal damnation."[28] As O'Connell points out, Stubbes has identified the *logos* of the gospel with the written word, rather than with the pre-existent Word who in time became flesh. It is a telling slip.

27. M. O'Connell, *The Idolatrous Eye: Iconoclasm and Theater in Early Modern England* (New York: Oxford University Press, 2000) p. 19. [Footnotes 27 and 28 have been updated for the 2005 edition of my book. –M.H.]

28. P. Stubbes, *The Anatomie of Abuses* (London, 1583) p. 102, quoted in O'Connell, op. cit., p. 29.

Barish traces "the anti-theatrical prejudice" in its various forms from Plato to the present day. We need not rehearse further the details that he has so amply documented. Enough has been said to demonstrate that our heritage, both classical and Christian, is one that, in Barish's words, confers "on the stage, and on theatricality in everyday life, the faint but unmistakable savor of forbidden fruit."[29] If the reader has, in the course of this book, felt some resistance to the idea of divine revelation having a theatrical cast, this may well be the reason. The written word is presumed to be "safer," its nature less sensual and its effect easier to control. But, as Barth often reminds us, the God of Jesus Christ is not ours to control. Perhaps it is appropriate that his choice of medium should unsettle us.

In Token of Endless Mirth

Disturbing though Christ's "theater" may have been, confusion turned to joy among those of his audience for whom the curtain was not closed on his death but "torn in two" (Matt. 27:51) and the sequel seen to be his resurrection. One would hope, therefore, to find in the history of the Church a redemptive vision that might find a place for "play" amidst the celebration. In *The Play Called Corpus Christi,* V. A. Kolve draws attention to what he calls "the most extensive defense of mirth within the Christian life that has survived from the English Middle Ages."[30] It is found in a work known as *Dives et Pauper,* written sometime between 1405 and 1410, and "offers a defense of the miracle plays specifically as a source of mirth and gladness."

During a discussion of the kinds of behavior proper on the Sabbath if the Third Commandment is to be obeyed, Dives asks whether miracle plays and dances are lawful on Sundays and great feast days. Pauper replies that when these be staged "principally for devotion, honesty and mirth, to teach men to love God the more," then there can be no objection. Surprised by the mention of mirth, Dives objects, "It seemeth by thy speech that in holidays men may lawfully make mirth."

29. Barish, op. cit., p. 477.

30. For what follows see Kolve, op. cit., pp. 131-34. I have modernized spelling and punctuation in quotations from *Dives et Pauper.*

Of course, Pauper responds, and quotes the Psalmist: "This is the day that God made. Make we now merry and be we glad" (Ps. 118:24). Dives, however, is well versed in the fulminations of the Church Fathers and quotes Augustine against dancing on Sunday. Pauper objects:

> Saint A[ug]ustin speaketh of such dances and plays as was used in his time when Christian people was much meddled with heathen people and by old custom and example of heathen people used unhonest dances and plays that by old time were ordained to stir folk to lechery and to other sins.

Pauper here readily acknowledges the power of the stage to influence for ill and agrees that if dances and plays now "stir men and women to pride, to lechery, gluttony and sloth," then they are no more lawful now than they were in the time of Augustine. "But against honest dances and plays done in due time and in good manner in the holiday spoke not Saint Austin."

So far the argument has produced nothing particularly unexpected. But Pauper goes on to argue that plays and dances that provoke honest mirth are particularly appropriate to Sundays. Knowing that "the hope, the desire and the longing that is delayed tormenteth the soul" (Prov. 13:12), God, he says, ordained the Sabbath as a present foretaste of the heaven to which we look forward. As we will rest in heaven, so on the Sabbath we are granted a token of that rest. Such rest from physical labor is both welcome in itself and a type of that "endless rest" anticipated by Christians. But heavenly rest will not be a kind of sedate lethargy. Rather it will be characterized by great "joy and mirth." And so, if the Sabbath is to be a true type of heaven, it too must be full of honest joy and mirth:

> Know it so that the rest, the mirth, the ease and the welfare that God hath ordained in the holidays is token of endless rest, joy and mirth and welfare in heaven's bliss that we hope to have without end.

Plays and dances that promote and give expression to such mirth are therefore to be particularly encouraged on Sabbaths and holidays. Kolve summarizes:

> Dismissing out of hand the ascetic argument for anguish and self-torment, [the author] assumes as self-evident that we all long for

> eternal rest and joy – the Sabbath of the world, the end of human time – and that longing deferred does us physical and spiritual harm. Therefore, he says, God, knowing this, has ordained a "figure" of that eternal rest for us, as a recurring medicine to our longing: the weekly Sabbath is our foretaste of the joy that will have no end. We honor it and God, and we do ourselves good, by celebrating it with mirth such as miracle plays and honest dances.

Although the author of *Dives et Pauper* refers to miracle plays, which were explicitly Christian in content, we must remember that these plays were never prim nor exclusively dogmatic. Although, as we have hinted in our earlier discussion of the juxtaposition of the cross and smithy in the Cornish *Ordinalia,* the comic in these plays complemented and reinforced the theological, it was still a thoroughly earthy humor. Pauper too applauds the enjoyment of dances, which could hardly have been instruments of indoctrination. The point is simply that it is godly to share mirth and that to do so in an "honest" manner in itself teaches us "to love God the more." If, in the process, the good news of the Christian kerygma is made explicit in plays, all well and good. But it is not necessary to Pauper's argument. Honest mirth is in itself token of heavenly joy and plays can generate such mirth.

Something akin to the mirth of which we have been speaking was found by Karl Barth in listening to the music of Mozart. Barth confessed to beginning each day not with study but with Mozart, explaining, "Our daily bread must also include playing. . . . And in Mozart I hear an art of playing as I hear it in no one else."[31]

Barth admits that the appeal of Mozart is hard to define, but suggests that it has to do with his willingness to embrace freely the whole range of human experience in his music:

> One marvels again and again how everything comes to expression in him: heaven and earth, nature and man, comedy and tragedy, passion in all its forms and the most profound inner peace, the Virgin Mary and the demons, the church mass, the curious solemnity of the Freemasons and the dance hall, ignorant and sophisticated people, cowards and heroes (genuine or bogus), the faithful and the

31. K. Barth, *Wolfgang Amadeus Mozart,* trans. C. K. Pott (Grand Rapids: Eerdmans, 1986) p. 16.

> faithless, aristocrats and peasants, Papageno and Sarastro. And he seems to concern himself with each of these in turn not only partially but fully; rain and sunshine fall on all.[32]

The extremes of sentimentality and gloom are precluded by such an embrace. But nor is this simply a "balanced" appraisal of humanity in which light and dark are found to coexist in perpetual equilibrium. On the contrary,

> What occurs in Mozart is rather a glorious upsetting of the balance, a *turning* in which the light rises and the shadows fall, though without disappearing, in which joy overtakes sorrow without extinguishing it, in which the Yea rings louder than the Nay.[33]

Mozart's music, for Barth, attests to the darkness and sorrow in human experience, but then, without in any way compromising that testimony, turns to the light which overwhelms it. "We will never hear in Mozart," Barth wrote, "an equilibrium of forces and a consequent uncertainty and doubt. . . . No matter how darkly foreboding" the beginning of a *Kyrie,* for example, by its end the music is "borne upward by the trust that the plea for mercy was granted long ago."[34] In this respect, Barth declared, Mozart "knew something about creation in its total goodness that neither the real fathers of the Church nor our Reformers," nor any theologian or musician before or since has known or been able to "express and maintain as he did."[35] Mozart, he concluded, offers us musical "parables of the realm of God's free grace as revealed in the gospel."[36] It is, after all, characteristic of the God of Jesus of Nazareth to offer startling parables!

Wimsatt and Beardsley would no doubt accuse Barth of indulging in the affective fallacy in his appreciation of Mozart. Mozart's music sounds a lot like Barth's theology. But the point here is not whether Barth was "correct" in his assessment of Mozart; rather, that the effect

32. Ibid., p. 34.
33. Ibid., p. 55.
34. Ibid., p. 56.
35. Barth, *CD,* 3/3, p. 298.
36. K. Barth, *How I Changed My Mind* (Richmond, Va.: John Knox Press, 1966) pp. 71-72.

of which he speaks, and which he felt was the best possible preparation for his daily work on the *Church Dogmatics,* is akin to that which the medieval author of *Dives et Pauper* felt to be so proper for the Christian celebrating the Sabbath and, in type, the mirth of heaven. In the second half of this book, we will consider the kinds of plays – and they will not by any means be all "Christian" – which are able to foster such a joyous affirmation of the time and space in which humanity finds itself.

But perhaps we should end this chapter by recalling the words given to Mozart in Peter Shaffer's *Amadeus.* You will remember that Mozart envisions "a finale lasting half an hour," beginning as a quartet but incorporating more and more singers all giving musical voice to their characters' several thoughts. Potential cacophony is blended by the music into multiple harmony. That, exults Mozart, must be "how God hears the world. Millions of sounds ascending at once and mixing in His ear to become an unending music, unimaginable to us!" The composer's job is to combine and set to music the inner thoughts of the widest possible range of people, from "chambermaids" to "Court Composers," and so "turn the audience into God."

It is, of course, an impossible vision. But the idea that an audience, instead of being enflamed with (and possibly purged of) passion or awakened to the nature of social evil, might be enabled by theater, in some measure, to see the world, warts and all, as, according to Barth, God sees it, with grace and good humor, and to respond to that vision with a mirth that is, whether the audience knows it or not, a foretaste of mirth yet in store, is an attractive proposition.

Chapter 5 Celebration and Escape

Theater's effect on an audience depends in part on the evaluative stance taken by a particular performance towards the worlds from which it draws its raw material and in which its audience lives. The same may be said of biblical parable, spoken or enacted, and indeed of "theatrical" or "incarnational" revelation in general. Thus far, with respect to the theater, we have considered predominantly formal relationships – between text and performance, between time and space on stage, between dramatic image and "real" world, and between performance and audience – and we have sought points of contact between these and parallel relationships in what the biblical witnesses understood to be God's mode of self-revelation. Now we turn from the manner of performance and revelation to the matter; specifically, to their respective assessments of human time and space, at once their medium and motif. For, in both the classical and Christian traditions, no less than in the modern theater, there is often found barring the way to that mirth of which we spoke in the last chapter, a deep suspicion of human time and space.

Animated Iconography

We can begin with a moment towards the end of *The Slaughter of the Innocents* which we passed over briefly in our first account of that play. While the resurrected Innocents are being welcomed into heaven, Herod dies. But he is not raised; he is "removed" and "his son Archelaus

. . . substituted in his place." Though theologically incomplete – Herod's soul was no doubt presumed bound for hell – the simultaneous resurrection of the Innocents and "removal" of Herod's corpse provides a telling dramatic effect. Herod has been the secular figure, focusing on temporal power and security; at death, his corpse is removed to rot in time. The Innocents have focused on eternity; they are raised to timeless bliss. The monks, whose own self-imposed exile from the secular world to the monastic contemplation of eternity has been one of the facets of reality imitated by the choirboy actors, are implicitly congratulated on the wisdom of their decision.

But this betrays a distrust of human time that, once it has been noted, is seen to permeate the play. Eternity is the dimension of blessedness; time is the dimension of cruelty, of sorrow and of death. In time, martyrs, Innocents and children of the Church are persecuted. The consolation offered to Rachel in her grief is that her "sons live blessed above the stars." Despite the Christmas season, the Incarnation of Christ in time and space is not stressed; rather the dominant image of Christ is that of the Lamb enthroned "for ever," receiving the praises of the Church, interceding for the sins of men, and welcoming the souls of the redeemed to his side in eternity. To be trapped in time is the fate of the villain; to be ushered into eternity is the reward of the followers of Christ.

Even in a play, then, that exhibits a magnificent vision of God's providential interweaving of the events of history to create a thick and multivalent tapestry of redemption, there is at bottom a deep-seated suspicion of human time and hankering after eternity. What is the source, in a play that might so easily have celebrated the affirmation of human time and space entailed in the Incarnation, of this longing for eternity? A hint may be contained in Richard Axton's apt description of liturgical drama as "animated iconography."[1] For the roots of the liturgical drama's artistic monasticism are in all likelihood entangled with those of the icon, the latter having their well-documented origin in a neo-Platonism mediated to the Church through Plotinus and pseudo-Dionysus.

According to Plotinus, man's fundamental metaphysical problem

1. R. Axton, *European Drama of the Early Middle Ages* (London: Hutchinson, 1974) p. 67.

is that he is finite, while God is infinite. If man would know God, he must approach him not through study but by a path that transcends the finite human mind. The mystic must pass beyond what he can perceive with his senses to contemplate the realm of "ideas." Yet higher and he will leave behind all rational thought and, though still self-conscious, unite with the Mind of the universe, in which truth is perceived intuitively. Thence he will press on to mystical union with God, an ecstasy from which all duality is finally absent.

Plotinus' mystical way was introduced into the Church, couched in Christian terminology, by the sixth-century writer known as pseudo-Dionysius. Dionysius suggested that union with God could be attained by contemplation of those images of God contained, first and most imperfectly, in the sensible world; then in the liturgy and ecclesiastical hierarchy of the Church; and thirdly, leaving behind the sensible world altogether, in the unseen celestial hierarchy of angels. The final step is to pass beyond images to the contemplation of and absorption into the otherwise unknowable God himself.

The importance of all this to icons and hence to liturgical drama stems from the neo-Platonic philosophy of icons developed under pressure of the iconoclastic controversy in the eighth and ninth centuries. The patriarch Nicephorus among others defended icons by incorporating them into pseudo-Dionysius' mystic way. Icons, he argued, offered to the worshipper, like the bread and wine of the Mass, "the tradition and the history of the Faith without mediation, the things themselves as though they were present." I. P. Sheldon-Williams comments, "There is here the implication that the image is more than a mere memorial of an archetype which is no longer there. The presence of the archetype in the image, though not substantial, is a real presence."[2] That is, the worshipper is contemplating not a mere work of art, an image of an image, but, let us say, the Madonna herself, really present in the icon. The icons therefore helped the spiritual pilgrim as he passed from contemplation of the sensible world to contemplation of celestial realms. The Madonna was no longer beyond the reach of his mind in heaven, but immediately present before him.

2. I. P. Sheldon-Williams, "The Greek Christian Platonist Tradition from the Cappodacians to Maximus and Eriugena," in *The Cambridge History of Later Greek and Early Medieval Philosophy* (Cambridge: Cambridge University Press, 1967) pp. 515-16.

The iconoclastic controversy was settled theoretically by the seventh Ecumenical Council at Nicaea in 787, where the veneration of images was officially encouraged. When Theodora, sympathetic to the use of icons, acceded to the regency of the Empire in 843, it was settled practically. The neo-Platonic aesthetic dominated: the purpose of the icon was to aid the congregation in contemplating and drawing nearer to the One in eternity.

The first liturgical plays date from this period. The earliest extant text comes from the eighth century,[3] and it may be no coincidence that it was not until the tenth century, by which time the edicts of the Council of Nicaea had been widely accepted in Western Europe, that the "animated iconography" of liturgical drama began properly to flourish. In any case, the liturgical plays, although not sharing the "supernatural efficacy"[4] of the icons, were created in the same aesthetic milieu. Thus the Fleury *Slaughter of the Innocents* focuses not on the actual massacre, as a modern film might, but on the Innocents as an emblem of martyred saints, on Rachel as an image of the Madonna and on the exalted Lamb. Herod, because he will not wrest his focus from human time and space, is removed to rot in a temporal and spatial grave; the choirboys and all whom they represent, because they have focused on eternity, are raised and welcomed into heaven.

Archaic Time

Such a distrust of time is not exclusive to the neo-Platonic Christianity of the monastery. Mircea Eliade has amply documented archaic man's "terror" of being "overwhelmed by the meaninglessness of profane" time and his determination to escape whenever possible to "sacred" or "mythical" time. This too has found its way into the theater, not only, as one might expect, in archaic ritual, but also in the theory and practice of the modern stage.

In *The Myth of the Eternal Return,* Eliade wrote of archaic man's be-

3. Axton, op. cit., p. 61.

4. M. H. Marshall, "Aesthetic Values of the Liturgical Drama," in J. Taylor and A. H. Nelson (eds.), *Medieval English Drama* (Chicago: University of Chicago Press, 1972) p. 33.

lief in *illo tempore,* a "mythical" or "sacred" time in which "the foundation of the world occurred" and the archetypal acts of gods, ancestors and heroes were first performed. Present man may enter sacred time by the ritual mimesis of such archetypal acts; and he may return to it, erasing the elapsed interval by means of New Year festivals and purification rites. In this way, profane time is abolished and "everything begins over again at its commencement every instant."[5]

Such language is now being used to describe the theatrical event. David Cole, for example, has compared the actor to a shaman who, as a representative of his tribe, visits the *illud tempus,* "the world of archetypal myth itself." Just as the shaman falls into "a trance during which his soul is believed to leave his body and ascend to the sky or descend to the underworld," so the actor, exploring the archetypal *illud tempus* of a script, begins his preparation for performance by making "a journey to his psychic interior" in search of "answering impulses, shared fantasies, common symbolisms." There then occurs what Cole calls a "rounding." The actor abandons the role of shaman, one sent by the tribe to the *illud tempus,* and takes on the role of hungan, one who, possessed by a spirit from the *illud tempus,* is sent from that realm back to his tribe. Cole explains this in psychological terms: "Hungan and actor both submit to being taken over by the rejected, and hence unconscious, aspects of their personalities." The actor, thus "possessed" by another personality from the *illud tempus,* an archetypal image of his own and his audience's repressed impulses, is able to make that hidden world physically present to the audience. Mimesis has conjured up archetypal reality; present play time has become archaic sacred time.[6]

Although David Cole judiciously defines the relationship of performance time and *illud tempus* in psychological terms, others are less inclined to demythologize. Peter Brook also believes that theatrical "representation denies time," abolishing the "difference between yesterday and today."[7] But it is "not for a bundle of repressed passions" that Brook aims to teach a performer "to become the vehicle." Rather,

5. M. Eliade, *The Myth of the Eternal Return* (Princeton: Princeton University Press, 1971) pp. 92, 20-21, 89.

6. D. Cole, *The Theatrical Event* (Middletown, Conn.: Wesleyan University Press, 1975) pp. 9, 17 (quoting Eliade), 22-23, 46.

7. Brook, op. cit., p. 126.

according to Ted Hughes, it is for spirits, "powers much closer to the source," in whose loss "the real distress of our world begins."[8]

In *The Empty Space,* Brook offered the possession ritual of Haitian voodoo as a model for a new "holy theatre." He described how, after "five or six hours" of drumming, chanting and drinking rum on the part of the human participants,

> the gods fly in. . . . Through the wood [of the ceremonial pole], earthed, the spirits slide. . . . Now they need a human vehicle, and they choose one of the participants. A kick, a moan or two, a short paroxysm on the ground and a man is possessed. He gets to his feet, no longer himself, but filled with the god. The god now has form. . . . He's a god all right, but he is no longer unreal: he is there, on our level, attainable. The ordinary man or woman can now talk to him, pump his hand, argue, curse him, go to bed with him – and so, nightly, the Haitian is in contact with the great powers and mysteries that rule his day.[9]

For his 1971 production of *Orghast,* a mythological text devised in collaboration with Ted Hughes, Brook's stated goal was to form the cast into a single "organism" that, once "possessed," would neither "teach" nor "explain," but "create a circle" with the audience "in which the [sacred] impulse can go round."[10] A description of the play's opening scene gives some idea of the nature of the performance. This was played, not in a conventional theater, but on a cliff face, 200 yards across and 200 feet straight up, just outside Persepolis in Iran. The performance began after sunset. Silhouetted on the skyline, a woman representing Light sang "a long, tremulous note" into the silence. From the distance, an actor representing Man answered with a guttural cry in Avesta, the sacred language of Zoroastrianism. Light sang again and this time Man's response was closer. Then the chorus, seated at ground level, in front of the audience but facing one another, began to chant "throaty, staccato murmurs, and swells, not in unison." Prometheus could be seen chained on a ledge high on the cliff face. Moa, another

8. T. Hughes, quoted in A. C. H. Smith, *Orghast at Persepolis* (New York: Viking, 1973) pp. 244-45.

9. Brook, op. cit., pp. 57-58.

10. Brook, quoted in Smith, op. cit., p. 200.

mythical figure, called to Prometheus from within an ancient burial chamber, hollowed out from the cliff face some 60 feet above the ground. Meanwhile Man had crawled onto the platform of this tomb. Now, over the edge of the cliff above and slowly rolling down it, there appeared a huge ball of fire. Man took the fire with a long, iron hook, set it in a bowl, and knelt before it in adoration.[11]

Critical reaction was mixed. The opera critic of the *Financial Times* was profoundly moved, concluding that "the playgoer who has entered deeply into *Orghast* has passed through fire, and can never be the same again." But the reviewer in *Theater Heute* disliked this "striking example of a movement in the theatre towards mystification, a flight from the everyday world into myth, ritual and meditation."[12] Disapprove as he may, he had understood the nature of the production well. For *Orghast* involved on a grand scale what Eliade calls "the abolition of time through the imitation of archetypes and the repetition of paradigmatic gestures."[13] Theatrically, it was, in many respects, a *tour de force;* philosophically, it was an instance of what Nathan Scott has called the "stifled panic" of the modern literary imagination in the face of time.[14]

Christian Time

Eliade has designated Plato as "the thinker who succeeded in giving philosophic currency and validity to the modes of life and behavior of archaic humanity";[15] and I have suggested that the aesthetics of liturgical drama may be traced to neo-Platonic roots. If both these insights are correct, it would seem that the archaic suspicion of human time found sophisticated philosophical expression in the writings of Plato and passed thence, through Plotinus and pseudo-Dionysius, into the Christian Church and its liturgical drama, reappearing in the modern theater in a form consciously reminiscent of its archaic original.

But there is another way of viewing human time and space. William Lynch, in his book *Christ and Apollo,* has written that "Christian

11. Smith, op. cit., pp. 200-202.
12. A. Porter and E. Wendt, quoted in ibid., pp. 236, 243.
13. Eliade, op. cit., p. 35.
14. N. A. Scott, *The Broken Center* (New Haven: Yale University Press, 1966) p. 40.
15. Eliade, op. cit., p. 34.

belief is in its essence belief in a Man who, having 'created' time, could not possibly be hostile to it," and who, in dramatic confirmation of the decision of Creation, "finally entered" human time and space as Jesus of Nazareth.[16] Such a rediscovery of the affirmation of human time and space implicit in the doctrines of Creation and Incarnation has been, according to Nathan Scott, one of the more refreshing features of modern theology. Scott, in 1966, professed to discern a "general movement in contemporary Christian thought" away from that "radical distinction between time and eternity that has persistently figured in theological tradition" and towards a positive re-evaluation of human time as the dimension to which, in Emil Brunner's words, God "pledged Himself" in Jesus Christ. "What is now beginning to be discovered," Scott wrote,

> is that the whole notion of time and eternity as radically disjunctive descends not from the distinctively Biblical sources of Christian tradition but rather from the Hellenic (and, more specifically, Platonist) background of patristic thought.

Among other theologians cited by Scott as having found, in "the strange new world within the Bible," cause to question "the Greek contrast between time and eternity" is Karl Barth.[17] As always, Barth grounds his thinking in the doctrine of the Incarnation:

> A correct understanding of the concept of eternity is reached only if we start . . . from the real fellowship between God and the creature, and therefore between eternity and time. This means starting from the incarnation of the divine Word in Jesus Christ. The fact that the Word became flesh undoubtedly means that, without ceasing to be eternity, in its very power as eternity, eternity became time.[18]

That God made human time and space and indeed the whole creation "as the theatre and instrument of His acts, an object of His joy and for

16. Lynch, op. cit., p. 50.

17. Scott, *The Broken Center,* pp. 58-59, 62; E. Brunner, "The Christian Understanding of Time," *Scottish Journal of Theology,* IV (1951) p. 8.

18. Barth, *CD,* 2/1, p. 616.

participation in His joy,"[19] and that, under the care of divine Providence, "creaturely history" continues to be "the theatre of the great acts of God,"[20] is part and parcel of Barth's faith. But it is the Incarnation that, for Barth, bespeaks a divine affirmation of human time far more radical even than that of Creation and Providence:

> What happens in Jesus Christ is not simply that God gives us time, our created time, as the form of our own existence and world, as is the case in creation and in the whole ruling of the world by God as its Lord. In Jesus Christ it comes about that God takes time to Himself, that he Himself, the eternal One, becomes temporal, that He is present for us in the form of our own existence and our own world, not simply embracing our time and ruling it, but submitting Himself to it, and permitting created time to become and be the form of His eternity.[21]

Far from inviting man, in other words, to escape time in order to be with God, God clothes himself in flesh and therefore in time in order to be with man. It is a question of Emmanuel, God with us in time, and not of mysticism, man with God outside time.

Barth is not blind to the sorrow and pain experienced by man in time. Christ above all suffered, and therefore testifies to "God's participation in [both] the splendour and misery of created being."[22] Nonetheless, God is revealed in Christ as the One who embraces man in his time, and time is shown to be the dimension given by God to man "for the history of the covenant between God and man." Far from being a hostile dimension, barring our way to a God who remains for ever secluded in the distant reaches of eternity, "this mighty ordinance of time . . . is as we receive and possess it" in the light of God's gracious intemporisation in Christ

> a hymn of praise to God, a proclamation of His mighty acts, the hidden rustling of the Holy Spirit, the garment and form of the grace in which God wills to meet us.[23]

19. Ibid., 3/1, p. 102.
20. Ibid., 3/3, p. 50.
21. Ibid., 2/1, p. 616.
22. Ibid., 3/1, p. 378.
23. Ibid., 3/2, pp. 526-27.

The Second Shepherds' Play

Not all religious theater turns away from human time to face eternity. The focus of the popular medieval cycle plays, for example, was on Christ's Incarnation and Passion in the midst of human history. While neither the reality of temporal suffering nor the promise of eternal joy was set aside, the plays accorded to the stuff of daily human life a dignity not found in the liturgical drama of the period. Perhaps this had to be if the plays were to be popularly performed not by monks but by successive generations of tradesmen and farmers.

The Second Shepherds' Play, from the fifteenth-century Wakefield cycle, is a good example. Three shepherds, Coll, Gib and Daw, meet on a bleak moor. They are, in all probability, indistinguishable from the laborers and shepherds in the audience with whom they were chatting and joking a moment before, and from whose midst they step forward to begin the play. Play time is present time. They complain, in broad Yorkshire dialect, of freezing weather, nagging wives and crippling taxes paid to the gentry. But they do so with a measure of self-deprecating good humor. Coll explains, with a sudden grin to the audience:

> It does me good, as I walk thus by mine own,
> Of this world for to talk in manner of moan. (46-47)[24]

Soon the shepherds are joined by Mak, a reputed sheep stealer, who grumbles about his poverty and his wife's fecundity. The four huddle together for warmth and go to sleep. But, during the night, Mak wakes, makes off with one of the sheep and carries it home to his wife, Gill. To escape detection, she hides it in the crib and, in the morning, when the shepherds arrive in pursuit of the missing sheep, pretends to have given birth to yet another son. The scene is thus both an amusing piece of local realism and a carefully contrived visual pun on the nativity story: three shepherds paying their respects to the newborn Lamb.

When the shepherds leave, all seems to be going well for Mak. But Daw regrets not giving a gift to the baby and returns with sixpence.

24. *The Second Shepherds' Play,* in Bevington (ed.), op. cit., pp. 383-408. I have again modernized medieval spelling.

Bending to kiss him, he notices that the baby has an abnormally long snout! The game is up. The shepherds retrieve their sheep and good-humoredly toss Mak in a blanket as punishment.

Back on the moor, an angel appears to the shepherds and announces Christ's birth in Bethlehem. Suddenly we are no longer in fifteenth-century Yorkshire but in first-century Judah. There has, however, been no shift in style. The shepherds whom angels visit and who travel to Bethlehem to present their gifts to the new-born Messiah are men like those in their audience. It was into such a world, different only in its accidents, that Christ came.

This easy mingling of divine and human time is perhaps best captured in the speeches made by the shepherds as they offer their gifts to the Christ child. They know that the baby is the Creator, he "that made all of nought" (721), and the Redeemer, to whom Daw prays, "Be near when that I have need" (729). But he is also a real human baby. They call him little moppet, and are delighted when he laughs:

> Lo, he merries,
> Lo, he laughs, my sweeting! (714-15)

They bring him gifts that any Wakefield man or woman might take a new-born child: a bob of cherries to hang over his crib, a caged song bird to appeal to his developing senses of sound and sight, and a tennis ball to grasp and roll around with his tiny, pudgy hands.

Gib's speech is perhaps the most extraordinary example of this interwoven delight in the child as a new-born creature and worship of him as Creator:

> Hail, sovereign Saviour, for thou hast us sought!
> Hail, frely foyde [noble child] and flower, that all thing has
> wrought!
> Hail, full of favour, that made all of nought!
> Hail! I kneel and I cower. A bird have I brought
> To my bairn.
> Hail, little tiny mop!
> Of our creed thou art crop.
> I would drink on thy cup,
> Little day-star. (719-27)

The "bairn" before whom Gib kneels is Creator of "all thing" and "sovereign Saviour" of mankind, and he is a "tiny moppet" who will enjoy the antics of the songbird.

The last two lines of Gib's speech are particularly rich. They work well on the level of good-natured adult prattle to a baby, and in this sense might be modernized as something like "I'll drink to you, my little sunshine!" But they work equally well as an expression of worship. "I would drink on thy cup" is borrowed from the biblical description of the Eucharist: "For as often as you eat this bread and drink the cup, you proclaim the Lord's death until he comes" (1 Cor. 11:26). On this level, Gib is promising to partake of the sacrament.

"Day-star" can be variously interpreted. Medieval preachers understood the day star to be "the time of grace." "Now is the day star up," one preacher told his congregation, adding, "I understand by the day star nothing else but this time, that is now time of grace."[25] The readers of the Second Epistle of Peter had been encouraged to pay heed to the "sure word of prophecy as unto a light that shineth in a dark place until the day dawn and the day star arise in your hearts" (2 Pet. 1:19 KJV). Elsewhere in the New Testament "the morning star" (Rev. 2:28, 22:16) and the synonymous "dayspring from on high" (Lk. 1:78 KJV) are titles accorded to Christ. On the level of doxology, therefore, Gib is rejoicing in the promised dawning of the Messianic day star, in history and in his own heart, and in the inauguration of the time of grace.

The Wakefield playwright has, in effect, written a speech that invokes the sweep of Christian history, from Creation through Incarnation, Passion and Church Sacrament, without once disrupting the playful naturalism of the shepherd's banter. It is entirely in keeping with the style of the play as a whole. In *The Second Shepherds' Play,* the Incarnation is located in the overall plan of redemption by the use of evocative scriptural language, secured in its true historical context by mention of the proper place names, and grounded in the quotidian reality of human living, not by archaeological precision, but by the very modernity of its details. Christ was born in history, to be sure, but it is a history of men and women like us. In the process, the essential dignity of man in time has been confirmed. For all its irritations, human

25. Quoted in Kolve, op. cit., p. 102.

life in time can be met with good humor and even joy in light of the fact that Christ chose to share and thereby to commend it.

Cyrano de Bergerac

There has been, to my knowledge, no tradition of theater since the medieval cycle plays in which human time has been so convincingly portrayed as at once fallen and of value. Indeed, at the risk of gross generalization, the intervening years on the stage might be characterized as one long attempt to hold at bay either the pain or the joy of human time. Rarely have a playwright's arms been wide enough to embrace them both.

Along the way, however, and by way of exception to the general rule, there have been individual plays that have caught something of the spirit of exuberance with which it is possible, even in a fallen world, to enjoy our time. Few if any of these are explicitly Christian in their orientation. But, as Nathan Scott suggests, "It may . . . be an important part of the Christian's vocation toward the literature of our period to cherish and to admire" any work in which there is found an "unquerulous acceptance of the irrevocable temporality of the human condition." Though not fully biblical, they may nonetheless provide "proximate models of health and sanity of spirit."[26]

One such play, from the beginning of the modern period, is Edmond Rostand's *Cyrano de Bergerac.* This may, at first sight, seem a surprising assertion. For Hollywood has shown us that the text of Cyrano may be profitably performed as a rather shallow romance interspersed with swashbuckling sword fights and heroic battle scenes. But it may also be played, more wisely, as a celebration of the tangible and variegated stuff of life to be found even in the shadow of that "very old acquaintance," death.[27]

Consider the first scene. The curtains open on the interior of the Théâtre de l'Hôtel de Bourgogne in 1640. On stage, therefore, we see a second stage, an open floor for standing room and, higher up, galleries

26. Scott, *The Broken Center,* pp. 68, 76.

27. E. Rostand, *Cyrano de Bergerac,* trans. B. Hooker (New York: Bantam, 1959) p. 183.

and boxes. Two cavaliers enter the empty hall and, being early, elect to practice their fencing. A pair of lackeys follow, make themselves comfortable on the floor and bring out a pack of cards and a set of dice. A guardsman flirts with a reluctant flower girl. While the three actions progress simultaneously, we hear snatches of dialogue. Thrusting, the first cavalier proclaims, "A hit!" From the card game, the second lackey announces the suit, "A club!" Beseeching, the guardsman requests "A kiss!"

Then a larger group of spectators arrive and, spreading their packages of food and bottles of Burgundy on the floor, begin to eat and drink. A citizen, entering with his son, observes with distaste, "Would you not think you were in some den of vice?" He points his cane at the gourmands, pronouncing them "drunkards." Then, in stepping back fastidiously, he trips over one of the fencing cavaliers. "Bullies!" he roars. He falls between the lackeys; they must be "Gamblers!" As he struggles to his feet, he bumps into the guardsman who is still trying for a kiss from the flower girl. "Good God!" he expostulates and "draws his son quickly away." "Here!" he mutters in high disapproval, "And to think, my son, that in this hall/They play Rotrou!" The son, cut from the same delicate cloth, agrees: "Yes father – and Corneille!" Rotrou, like Corneille, was the author of highly proper neoclassical tragedies. It is a wonderful touch to invoke their names at this moment, contrasting so vividly the reality of this rather amiable "den of vice" with the unreal propriety of the neo-classical stage. Rostand has served notice that it is his mission neither to escape nor to disapprove the mundane pastimes of Parisian humanity.

More theatergoers enter: pages, to sit "up in the gallery" and with "a bit of string" and a hook, to "fish for wigs"; a pickpocket instructing his gang of apprentices; several orders of nobility; Corneille himself and the dignitaries of the French Academy; the "elaborately dressed" ladies, bowing and smiling as they enter their boxes; and finally, amidst a "sudden hush," His Eminence Cardinal Richelieu. It is a scene constructed with the same kind of appreciation for simultaneous action as we found in the Palm Sunday episode from the Cornish *Ordinalia*. Action is going on everywhere: in the galleries and in the boxes, on the increasingly crowded floor and even, though the curtains are still closed, on stage. To take just one of a rapid succession of instances: several marquis have seated themselves on stage to watch the action close up but discover they are a chair short. One of their number suddenly puts his head through the curtains, makes his need known, and "a chair is passed from hand to hand over the heads of the crowd." Blowing kisses to the ladies in the boxes, he disappears behind the curtains with his prize. Here, as throughout the scene, our eyes dart from one point to the next, scaling the heights and plumbing the depths of the physical theater on stage and the social classes gathered there, as Rostand's carefully wrought montage of dialogue and action directs us.

Almost incidentally, as we revel in this kaleidoscope of Parisian humanity, we are introduced to individuals who will play an important part in the action: Cyrano's cousin, Roxane, who inspires "murmurs of admiration" as she enters her box; the young baron, Christian de Neuvillette, newly arrived in the city and already enamoured of Roxane; Ragueneau, the rotund pastry-cook; and Cyrano himself, a young cadet already renowned as a poet and swordsman of impeccable integrity, fierce pride and astonishing ugliness. Perched in the center of his face is a nose so large that, as he says himself, it "marches on/ Before me by a quarter of an hour!"

Cyrano and his nose may serve as an emblem of Rostand's attitude to humankind in this play. To use theological language, the divine curse on Nature is emblazoned, bulbous and variegated, on Cyrano's face; in others human flaw manifests itself more discreetly, in theft, jealousy and self-righteousness. But the image of God survives, in Cyrano's unselfish love of Roxane and Christian, in Ragueneau's prodigal generosity, even in the drunken Lignière's trust in Cyrano's protection from his enemies. Rostand looks on man in his time, for all his deformity, with genuine affection.

Consider, by way of further illustration of Rostand's affirmation of human life, the theme of food in the play. After Cyrano has stopped the show at the Hôtel de Bourgogne and, in a splendid "gesture," flung his purse to the stage manager to reimburse the public, he has no money. The flower girl shyly offers to give him some of the food she has for sale. Though too proud to accept charity, he is too sensitive to offend: he selects a grape, a glass of water and half a macaroon, kisses the flower girl's hand "as he would the hand of a princess," and treats the meagre spread as he would a banquet.

Delight in a little does not preclude delight in a lot. Act Two begins with a wonderfully extravagant stage direction. Readers should imagine performance: what they would see and smell and hear and what the actors would taste on stage. The curtain opens on Ragueneau's bakery:

> In the foreground, at the Left, a Counter is surmounted by a Canopy of wrought iron from which are hanging ducks, geese, and white peacocks. Great crockery jars hold bouquets of common flowers, yellow sunflowers in particular. On the same side farther back, a huge fireplace; in front of it, between great andirons, of which each one supports a little saucepan, roast fowls revolve and weep into their dripping-pans. . . . In the centre of the shop, an iron ring hangs by a rope over a pulley so that it can be raised or lowered; adorned with game of various kinds hung from it by hooks, it has the appearance of a sort of gastronomic chandelier. . . . In the shadow under the staircase, ovens are glowing. The spits revolve; the copper pots and pans gleam ruddily. Pastries in pyramids. Hams hanging from the rafters. The morning baking is in progress: a bustle of tall cooks and timid scullions and scurrying apprentices; a blossoming of white caps adorned with cock's feathers or the wings of guinea-fowl. On white trays or on great metal platters they bring in rows of pastries and fancy dishes of various kinds.

Such a scene should be staged with abandon, so as to thrill the senses of the audience.

But it is not a feast of the gods, spared the effects of the Fall. Ragueneau is an aspiring poet, who composes recipes in rhyme and holds open house for the poets of Paris. His business suffers from his enthusiasm. So does his marriage. His wife, Lise, exasperated by his infatuation with the muse, flirts with musketeers. As he so often does, Rostand undercuts his extravagance with irony. At the beginning of the Third Act, the audience learns of Ragueneau's cuckolding and bankruptcy:

> – And so she ran off with a Musketeer!
> I was ruined – I was alone – Remained
> Nothing for me to do but hang myself,
> So I did that. Presently along comes
> Monsieur de Bergerac, and cuts me down,
> And makes me steward to his cousin.

The lady to whom he is talking protests:

> Ruined? –
> I thought your pastry was a great success!

Shaking his head in self-reproach, Ragueneau replies:

> Lise loved the soldiers, and I loved the poets –
> Mars ate up all the cakes Apollo left;
> It did not take long.

But, in Rostand's world, the collapse of the business does not invalidate the sensual pleasure in the pastries while they lasted. Human time entails both pain and pleasure; neither should be denied.

There is a final feast, a sensual surprise at the battle front. The company of guards to which Cyrano and Christian belong are part of the French army besieging Arras. They are in turn surrounded by Spanish troops and therefore cut off from all supply of food. Act Four begins with the cadets complaining of their empty bellies. Not only are they hungry but the imminent Spanish assault is anticipated at the point in the line that they are guarding: most of Cyrano's company can expect to lay down their lives in the ensuing battle.

Suddenly and unexpectedly a coach enters the camp "at full trot." To everybody's astonishment, Roxane descends. Embracing Christian, she explains that she broke through the Spanish lines by appealing to Spanish gallantry: whenever she was stopped, she would lower her eyes, murmur that she had a lover and find that she was allowed to pass. It is, we think, a triumph of romance, and Rostand allows ample time for the joy of reunion and the renewal of courage to be celebrated.

But Roxane announces that she is hungry after her journey, and the cadets are dismayed at their inability to provide. Sweetly Roxane orders her coachman to unpack. To our delight, the coachman turns out to be Ragueneau and the coach that has just ridden unstopped through Spanish lines to be stuffed with the finest of foods. Ragueneau, "standing on his box, like a mountebank before a crowd," produces, from various hiding places in the coach, roast fowl, a juicy ham and peacock *aux truffes.* "The cushions are eviscerated" to produce bottles of wine, the lamps of the carriage turn out to be *"bonbonnières,"* Ragueneau's "whip-handle is one long sausage," and so on. Roxane's journey through the Spanish lines has been not only an impractical triumph of romance but an ingenious triumph of practicality: she has broken the siege with much needed and highly delectable supplies. Pouring the wine and passing the food, she encourages the cadets, "We/ Being about to die, first let us dine!" It is not the feasting of those who pretend they will not die tonight, but of those who, knowing they may die, want once more to enjoy God's goodness on earth.

Cyrano's own death 15 years later – for he survives the battle – displays a similar wisdom. Sitting outdoors with Roxane, knowing he is dying, he watches the leaves fall:

> Yes, – they know how to die. A little way
> From the branch to the earth, a little fear
> Of mingling with the common dust – and yet
> They go down gracefully – a fall that seems
> Like flying!

As he feels "the great cold/ Gather round my bones," he is still able to laugh at death ("I can see him there – he grins – / He is looking at my nose – that skeleton") and to rejoice in a life that has been worth the living. Though Cyrano is properly allowed the final gesture, a celebration of the white plume of "freedom" that he wears in his hat and which he bears "unspotted from the world," a note of grace had been gently struck earlier in the scene. Some young nuns, loving Cyrano, had worried aloud that "he is not a good Catholic" and that they hoped to "convert him." Their Mother Superior had forbad them to try: "You need not/ Be afraid. God knows all about him." To be sure, this is not an end that preaches "Jesus Christ and him crucified" (1 Cor. 2:2), but it is an end that, like the play as a whole, proclaims both man's ability to accept his life and death in time and God's gracious willingness to accept man in his fallenness.

Chapter 6 Rough and Holy

Sir Philip Sidney complained of the early Elizabethan stage "mingling kings and clowns" in a form of "mongrel tragicomedy."[1] More than a century later, Joseph Addison shared with the urbane readers of *The Spectator* his conviction that "the tragi-comedy . . . is one of the most monstrous inventions that ever entered into a poet's thoughts."[2] It is striking, therefore, that Barth applauded Mozart's free embrace of "comedy and tragedy, . . . aristocrats and peasants"[3] and that the two plays advanced in the last chapter as affirmations of human life in its hardship and its joy are both, if they may be fitted at all to the classical genres, tragicomedies. Rostand designated *Cyrano de Bergerac* "an heroic comedy" and *The Second Shepherds' Play* happily mingled common shepherds and the King of kings. By offering these as "proximate models of health and sanity of spirit," we enter one of the long-standing debates of theatrical aesthetics.

There is, on the one hand, the neo-classical insistence on the separation of styles, confining vulgarity to comedy and nobility to tragedy. Aristotle had observed, on the Athenian stage, a clear distinction between the two. Tragedy, he wrote, represents "noble actions and the doings of noble persons"; comedy, being "more trivial," depicts "the meaner sort of people" (*Poetics,* ch. 4). Classical observation became neo-classical dogma. "Comedy," stipulated J. C. Scaliger, should employ "characters

1. P. Sidney, *An Apology for Poetry,* in Adams (ed.), op. cit., p. 174.
2. J. Addison, *The Spectator,* XXXIX (14 April 1711), in Clark (ed.), op. cit., p. 227.
3. Barth, *Wolfgang Amadeus Mozart,* p. 34; cf. above, pp. 74-75.

from rustic, or low city life" and its "language" be that of "everyday life"; "tragedy, on the other hand," should depict "kings and princes" and its language be "grave, polished, removed from the colloquial."[4]

On the other hand, however, there is the mixed style of the Jacobean theater, in which king and clown, Lear and Fool, Isabella and Overdone, nunnery and brothel, blank verse and bawdy prose, share the same world. Samuel Johnson acknowledged "the censure which [Shakespeare] has incurred by mixing comic and tragic scenes," but, he added, "there is always an appeal open from criticism to nature": "the real state of sublunary nature . . . partakes of good and evil, joy and sorrow," and ours is a world

> in which, at the same time, the reveler is hasting to his wine, and the mourner burying his friend; in which the malignity of one is sometimes defeated by the frolic of another.

Hence, he argued, the propriety of "the mingled drama."[5]

Although this is, on the surface, a debate about form, it entails, more profoundly, an evaluation of human life. If nothing else, neoclassicism assumes that nobility and vulgarity are easily distinguishable; the Christian, remembering that the Son of God was born in a stable and perhaps soiled his swaddling clothes in the presence of the magi, hesitates before that assumption. Put another way, the separation of styles bespeaks an impulse to regard everything about us that is, in Martha Nussbaum's phrase, "rooted in the dirt and standing helplessly in the rain" as an embarrassment, staining the "something about us that is pure."[6] The mixed style allows the possibility that nobility may play in the mud without disgrace and that shepherds may visit the Christ without presumption.

In Middleton's *A Mad World, My Masters,* Sir Bounteous Progress boasts of the fashionably genteel curtains on his four-poster bed:

> The curtains indeed were wrought in Venice, with the story of the prodigal child in silk and gold; only the swine are left out, my lord, for spoiling the curtains. (II, ii)

4. J. C. Scaliger, *Poetics,* in Clark (ed.), op. cit., p. 61.

5. S. Johnson, *Preface to Shakespeare,* in Adams (ed.), op. cit., p. 331.

6. Nussbaum, op. cit., p. 2.

That neo-classical weavers should feel obliged to omit swine from the biblical narrative in the interests of artistic decorum sums up the distinction well: for those who commissioned the Venetian weavers, pigs are an embarrassment; in the parable ascribed to Jesus of Nazareth, they are not. A consideration of style, therefore, both on stage and in the events and language of Scripture, will not merely advance our understanding of form but will further our discussion, begun in the previous chapter, of evaluative stance.

Neo-classical and Jacobean

There is a fastidiousness in neo-classical aesthetics that betrays a profound distaste for what William Lynch has called "the finite and limited concretions of our human life."[7] For all the talk of *vraisemblance,* life in a neo-classical tragedy is uncharacteristically refined. Bodily functions, even those as innocent as eating and sleeping, are rarely mentioned, let alone acted. Violence takes place off stage, and is then reported in stately alexandrine verse; polished speech, not physical action, is the medium of this theater. A neo-classical dramatist would have viewed with horror the kind of scene we admired earlier in the Cornish *Ordinalia:* lust at the smithy and crucifixion at Calvary. The scurrilous language of the torturer and the blacksmith's wife would be too vulgar for serious art; the crucifixion should never be staged, "since the audience . . . will always know that a killing on stage, and much more a crucifixion, is a faked effect"[8] and to juxtapose the two would be the most grotesque lapse of taste.

This formal restraint was part and parcel of the seventeenth century attempt to win, by human resolve, what Pascal called "la guerre intestine de l'homme entre la raison et les passions."[9] Corneille's alexandrine couplets triumph over common speech as *vertu* triumphs over passion. In *Polyeucte,* a woman married against her will but now willing

7. Lynch, op. cit., p. xiii.

8. J. de la Taille, "De l'art de la tragédie," 1572, paraphrased in Brereton, op. cit., p. 12.

9. "The war in the human gut between reason and the passions"; quoted in M. Turnell, *The Classical Moment* (London: Hamish Hamilton, 1947) p. 14.

fidelity, grants to the man she loved first and whom she still loves a carefully worded explanation of her outward coolness:

> Ma raison, il est vrai, dompte mes sentiments;
> Mais, quelque autorité que sur eux elle ait prise,
> Elle n'y règne pas, elle les tyrannise;
> Et quoique le dehors soit sans émotion,
> Le dedans n'est que trouble et que sédition. . . .
> Mais ce même devoir qui le vainquit dans Rome,
> Et qui me range ici dessous les lois d'un homme,
> Repousse encore si bien l'effort de tant d'appas
> Qu'il déchire mon âme et ne l'ébranle pas.
> C'est cette vertu même, à nos désirs cruelle,
> Que vous louiez alors en blasphémant contre elle:
> Plaignez-vous-en encor, mais louez sa rigueur,
> Qui triomphe à la fois de vous et de mon coeur. (II, ii)

> [My reason, it is true, controls my feelings,
> But whatso'er its mastery over them,
> It rules them by compulsion, like a tyrant,
> And though I give no outward sign thereof,
> Within me all is turmoil and rebellion. . . .
> But that same sense of duty which withstood thee
> In Rome and gave me to a husband here,
> Again so well resists thy dear attractions
> That though my soul is torn, it is not shaken.
> 'Tis the same virtue, cruel to our desires,
> Which thou didst praise of old, while railing at it.
> Lament it still, but praise its resolution,
> Which triumphs at once o'er thee and o'er my heart.][10]

Racine's verse, on the other hand, often expresses the control of the poet alone and not of his characters. Phèdre, despite months of relentless effort, is unable to suppress her lust for Hippolytus: *vertu*, though still exalted by reason, falls before the assault of passion. But if

10. *The Chief Plays of Corneille,* trans. L. Lockert (Princeton: Princeton University Press, 1957) pp. 235-36. The translation is, of course, in blank verse and not alexandrine couplets.

vertu fails, form keeps chaos at bay: never does the alexandrine skip a beat nor a comic indignity intrude, never a vulgar word is spoken nor a bloody action staged. The triumph of irresistible passion is portrayed in ordered alexandrines and with proper neo-classical decorum.

Human time and space are, from the neo-classical perspective, dimensions of the onslaught of passion. The tragic playwrights of the period escaped to an artificial world of play time and theatrical place, ordered, as off stage time and space are not, according to classical unities and in which, if *vertu* fails, poetic discipline succeeds. From such a world comic delight in human weakness and emotional untidiness is necessarily banned.

Shakespeare was no less aware of the struggle between virtue and passion. In *Measure for Measure,* negligent government has allowed Vienna to sink into moral disarray. Angelo, known for his virtue, is charged, in the Duke's absence, with the restoration of order. He sentences Claudio to death for fornication but, to his astonishment, is overcome with passion for Isabella when she pleads for her brother's life. He offers to exchange Claudio's pardon for Isabella's virtue. Isabella declines, preferring strict chastity to a stained charity. The plot as such would have appealed to neo-classical taste, and had in fact already formed the basis of an Italian tragedy, Giraldi's *Epizia.* But Shakespeare accords it an entirely different treatment. The action moves from palace to brothel, from prison to nunnery, the language from rich poetry to vulgar prose.

Peter Brook, who has twice directed *Measure for Measure,*[11] has described the play in terms of what he calls Rough and Holy. "The Rough Theatre," he writes,

> is close to the people. . . . Its arsenal is limitless: the aside, the placard, the topical reference, the local jokes, the exploiting of accidents, the songs, the dances, the tempo, the noise, the relying on contrasts, the shorthand of exaggeration, the false noses, the stock types, the stuffed bellies. . . . Its audience . . . has no difficulty in accepting inconsistencies of accent and dress, or in darting between mime and dialogue, realism and suggestion.

11. In 1950, for the Royal Shakespeare Company, and in 1979, at the Bouffes du Nord, Paris.

It is obscene and it is often aggressive, "anti-authoritarian, anti-pretence," a theater of laughter and rebellion. The Holy Theatre, by contrast, is a theater of rite and ceremony, soaring poetry and arcane language, having its origins in "rituals that made the invisible incarnate."[12]

For the most part, the two remain antagonistic. But in *Measure for Measure,* Brook claims, they combine forces with great power and must both be given full scope. With respect to the Rough, there must be no squeamishness in the brothel scenes, no sanitization of the prison. In his 1950 production for the Royal Shakespeare Company, an extraordinary array of inmates, crippled, deformed and violent, filled the Vienna gaol. At the same time, with regard to the Holy, the emotionally charged confrontations between Angelo and Isabella must be played with delicacy and restraint:

> When this play is prettily staged, it is meaningless – it demands an absolutely convincing roughness and dirt. . . ; and at the same time we must take great care, for all around the popular scenes are great areas of the play that clumsiness could destroy.

For Brook, the moment of greatest "holiness" comes in the final scene when Angelo, his sin uncovered, is publicly sentenced to death. Isabella, who had earlier pleaded with Angelo to temper justice with mercy in imitation of Christ (II, ii, 74-79), is now asked to plead for Angelo. In 1950 Brook asked the actress playing Isabella to pause at this point "until she felt the audience could take it no longer," and only then to kneel in intercession. On occasion there would be total silence and immobility for as much as two minutes. Brook writes:

> The device became a voodoo pole – a silence in which all the invisible elements of the evening came together, a silence in which the abstract notion of mercy became concrete for that moment to those present.

And yet this "voodoo pole" was only possible because it was rooted in "the disgusting, stinking world of medieval Vienna": "Isabella's plea for grace has far more meaning in this Dostoevskian setting than it would in lyrical comedy's never-never land" or, one

12. Brook, op. cit., pp. 60-61, 40.

might add, in the refined world of neo-classical tragedy, in which no concession to passion can be forgiven."[13] It is in the real world that grace is needed and, the Christian claims, into which it came. *Measure for Measure* recognizes that need and dramatizes it, flinching from neither dirt nor purity, calling for both the restraint of justice and the grace of mercy.

I suggested earlier that we might better appreciate Christ's ministry of grace if we were to reproduce in graphic detail on the mental stage of our imagination the cripples whom he touched and the underworld of prostitutes and sinners with whom he mixed. A properly rough and holy production of *Measure for Measure* points our imagination in that direction, not because, as some have claimed, either the Duke or Isabella are "Christ figures" but because, in the midst of human mismanagement, self-righteousness, decadence and disease, grace somehow shines and partially transforms both the world and our perception of it.

A Rough and Holy King

This mixture of Rough and Holy, which Brook finds so impressive in Shakespeare, has its roots deep in the Christian drama of the Middle Ages. And, as Erich Auerbach has so ably pointed out, this in turn has its roots in the doctrine of the Incarnation:

> The true heart of the Christian doctrine – Incarnation and Passion – was . . . totally incompatible with the principle of the separation of styles. Christ had not come as a hero and king but as a human being of the lowest social station. His first disciples were fishermen and artisans; he moved in the everyday milieu of the humble folk of Palestine; he talked with publicans and fallen women, the poor and the sick and the children. Nevertheless, all that he did and said was of the highest and deepest dignity, more significant than anything else in the world. The style in which it was presented possessed little if any rhetorical culture in the antique sense; it was *sermo piscatorius* and yet it was extremely moving and much more impres-

13. Ibid., pp. 80-81; J. C. Trewin, *Peter Brook* (London: Macdonald, 1971) pp. 53-55.

> sive than the most sublime rhetorico-tragical literary work. And the most moving account of all was the Passion. That the King of Kings was treated as a low criminal, that he was mocked, spat upon, whipped, and nailed to the cross — that story no sooner comes to dominate the consciousness of the people than it completely destroys the aesthetics of the separation of styles; it engenders a new elevated style, which does not scorn everyday life and which is ready to absorb the sensorily realistic, even the ugly, the undignified, the physically base. Or — if anyone prefers to have it the other way around — a new *sermo humilis* is born, a low style such as would properly only be applicable to comedy, but which now reaches out far beyond its original domain, and encroaches upon the deepest and the highest, the sublime and the eternal.[14]

Auerbach has properly stressed the juxtaposition of common life and elevated theme in the gospel. There is also, though less often noticed, comedy. The cleansing of the Temple, dramatized in the Cornish *Ordinalia,* is in Scripture too an example of the interweaving of classes and styles, of serious intent and comic effect. The King of kings enters Jerusalem humbly on a donkey. In holy anger at the blasphemy of the traders in the Temple, he creates what must have been a scene of high comedy: overturned tables, coins rolling down the temple steps, pompous merchants in total disarray scampering and groveling after their wealth and wares, excited pigeons freed, flapping and no doubt defecating on the chaos below. No wonder the children, who instinctively delight in adult deflation, cried out in delighted praise of this kind and comic King. The scribes and Pharisees protested as much the mixed style as the perceived blasphemy of the children's exuberance. Christ defended both style and content, calling it "perfect praise" (Matt. 21:16).

In the Fourth Gospel, the cleansing of the temple is placed earlier in the narrative and immediately preceded by the marriage at Cana. This makes for a gloriously comic chapter. Imagine a first-century counterpart of Bruegel's *Peasant Wedding.* There is a flurry of whispering at the head table. Servants scurry back and forth; the embarrassing news that the wine has run out must be kept from the guests at all costs. Mary notices the commotion and nudges Jesus. He grins and in-

14. Auerbach, op. cit., p. 72.

dicates their full glasses: "My dear lady, what's that to us. I'm not on call right now." Laughing, she tells the servants to do whatever he says. Near the entrance stand six huge stone jars, at once menial and pretentious: from them water has earlier been poured into basins so that the wedding guests could ceremonially wash their hands before eating (cf. Mark 7:1-4). Jesus chooses these as his props, telling the servants to refill them. Water is hurried to the jars by servants trying as hard as possible to evade guests asking for more wine. Jesus sits calmly. At last some of the water is drawn and taken to "the steward of the feast." Astonishment! The water has become "good wine." The steward rushes to the bridegroom to commend him for saving the best till last; the bridegroom is bewildered by the comment, the servants astonished and delighted. Jesus grins broadly at his mother. And in this way, the apostle comments, "Jesus manifested his glory" (Jn. 2:11). How different from the *gloire* of a neo-classical hero, won by iron-willed restraint!

The life and death of Christ are not the only biblical testimony to God's adoption of a mixed style in which to express his love for humanity. Consider the good humor of Creation, that God should make not only horse and hawk but ostrich and hippopotamus (Job 39:13–40:24) and playfully offer each of these to Adam as suitable "helpers" before producing woman (Gen. 2:18-23). Oliver O'Donovan has also reminded us that the bodily resurrection of Christ "tells us of God's vindication of his creation, and so of our created life":

> Before God raised Jesus from the dead, the hope that we call "gnostic," the hope for redemption *from* creation rather than for the redemption *of* creation, might have appeared to be the only possible hope.

Human rebellion might have appeared to have irreparably damaged God's good handiwork. But "in the resurrection of Christ creation is restored and the kingdom of God dawns" not outside but within human time and space.[15]

The resurrection too is played in mixed style in the biblical account. The risen Christ makes his first appearance in the borrowed costume of a gardener (Jn. 20:15), mischievously travels incognito to

15. O. O'Donovan, *Resurrection and the Moral Order* (Leicester: InterVarsity Press, 1986) pp. 13-15.

Emmaus while giving two of his despondent followers a comprehensive Bible study (Lk. 24:13-31), eats broiled fish (Lk. 24:42) and cooks a breakfast of fish and bread over an outdoor charcoal fire (Jn. 21:9-12). No neo-classical hero would have dreamed of stooping to such mundane activities.

Then there is the language of Scripture. Before the proliferation of modern translations, children giggled over the KJV use of "pisseth." Nonetheless I am persuaded that the Jacobean translators were correct, and that their successors have succumbed to post-Victorian squeamishness. He "that pisseth against the wall" (2 Kings 9:8 KJV) is obviously "male" (RSV), but something of the Jewish chronicler's choice of rough and holy has been lost in the euphemism.

Mankind and the Play of Adam

The Christian story was, in Auerbach's view, so alien to the classical separation of styles that, as the influence of the gospel spread, the classical aesthetic became untenable. The "Christian mixture of styles"[16] which replaced it flourished most luxuriantly, he believed, in the theater of the Middle Ages.

As an early and rich example of the mixed theatrical style, Auerbach offers, in *Mimesis,* the anonymous twelfth-century *Jeu d'Adam.* Here a choir sings, God speaks to Adam and Eve, devils bang cauldrons and kettles together, blow clouds of smoke from a lurid hell mouth and run amok among the audience. Adam and Eve are given the manners and language of a contemporary French burgher and his wife, the one "upright but not very brilliant," the other "vain and ambitious" and "deceived by an unscrupulous swindler." "The ancient and sublime occurrence" thus becomes "immediate and present," "the starting point of the Christian drama of redemption" is rendered as "a scene of simplest, everyday reality."[17] To use Brook's terms, the holy takes place in the midst of the recognizably rough.

Le Jeu d'Adam would certainly repay further comment. But it may be more to our purpose at this point to turn to a play that combines

16. Auerbach, op. cit., p. 73.
17. Ibid., p. 151.

boisterous obscenity and gracious mercy to a degree that strikingly foreshadows *Measure for Measure.* The anonymous fifteenth-century morality play *Mankind* can be thought of as a battle between two dramatic forms, sermon and folk play, over a third, a play of Adam. The play begins with Mercy, dressed as a priest, delivering a sermon to the audience. The theology is cheerful – he speaks of God as "the very founder and beginner of our first creation" (1) and of Christ as "this blessed prince that our nature doth glorify" (15)[18] – but the manner of delivery is pompous and, if he is to be allowed to continue, promises tedious theater. His sermon is interrupted, no doubt to the audience's delight, by Mischief, who mimics the preacher's rhyme scheme (42-47), mocks his exegesis (55-63) and accuses him, in terms borrowed from the traditional English folk play, of being big-headed (47).[19]

At this point, there is a leaf missing from the folio, during which presumably Mischief leaves and Mercy continues his sermon. When the manuscript resumes, Mercy is again interrupted, this time by the fashionable New Guise, Nowadays and Nought, who claim to have heard Mercy summon them (111) – probably he named them as contemporary dangers in the missing leaf – and who break into his sermon with "minstrels" and a "common dance" (71). When Mercy admonishes the intruders to "do way [stop]" their "revels," Nowadays reminds him to stick to his own script:

> Do way, good Adam? do way?
> This is no part of thy play. (82-84)

Two "plays" are fighting for possession of the audience and the folk actors insist that, if Mercy is to depart from his prepared text, it should not be to rebuke them but to join their dance. Understandably he refuses and the vices, having also failed to persuade him to translate obscenities into Latin, leave. For the moment, the sermon, temporarily disrupted by folk-players on their rounds, has stood its ground.

18. *The Macro Plays,* ed. M. Eccles, EETS 262 (London: Oxford University Press, 1969) pp. 153-84. I have modernized spelling and occasionally vocabulary in quoting from this text.

19. Cf. the opening lines of Big Head in the English folk play tradition: "Here comes I, that never come yet/ With great head and little wit"; E. K. Chambers, *The English Folk-Play* (Oxford: Clarendon Press, 1933) pp. 48, 64, 135.

But there is another interruption, this time more acceptable to homiletical Mercy. Mankind enters and is instructed by Mercy in the ways of piety. His sermon concluded, Mercy leaves Mankind obediently digging and sowing, in the manner of fallen Adam in *Le Jeu d'Adam.*[20] Sermon has yielded willingly to a bowdlerized Adam play, shorn of its devils and its comedy, and starring a distinctly smug Adam. Mankind congratulates himself on his "incomparable," "glorious" and "noble" estate and on having already triumphed over sin:

> Now blessed be Jesu! my soul is well satiate
> With the mellifluous doctrine of this worshipful man.
> The rebellion of my flesh now it is overcome. (311-13)

The folk players will have none of this. Adam must yield to the demonic and the comic. Making use of the traditional folk-play opening line, "Make room, sirs" (331),[21] they take immediate possession of the audience, inviting all present "to sing . . . with a merry cheer" a vulgar "Christmas song":

> It is written with a coal,
> He that shitteth with his hole,
> But he wipe his arse clean,
> On his britches 't shall be seen. (331-43)

They then turn their satire to the props of the Adam play. Performing indoors, mankind would have used just a spade and a small piece of sacking to simulate sowing and tilling. Nought stares at the sacking: "How many acres suppose ye here by estimation?" (360); and suggests that if Mankind lack rain, he can easily provide it: "If he will have rain he may overpiss it" (373). Mankind finally loses his patience and breaks out of the Adam play, attacking the folk-players/vices with his spade. The latter flee, Nought struck on the arm, Nowadays on the head and New Guise in the family "jewels": "Alas, my jewels," he moans, "I'll be scolded by my wife!" (381).

20. Cf., in *Le Jeu d'Adam,* "Then Adam shall have a spade and Eve a mattock and they shall begin to cultivate the ground and they shall sow wheat in it"; *Medieval French Plays,* trans. R. Axton and J. Stevens (Oxford: Basil Blackwell, 1971) p. 33.

21. Cf. Chambers, op. cit., pp. 16-19.

While Mankind leaves to fetch corn, Mischief "heals" the wounded Vices by means of a mock beheading and castration, promising both Nowadays and New Guise, "I can chop it off and make it again" (445). The operation again ties the vices to the traditional folk play, being reminiscent of both the Cure in a Mummers' Play and the beheading at the close of a sword dance.[22] In a production of *Mankind* in Cambridge in June 1969, the identity of Nowadays' head and New Guise's "privates" was stressed by a series of tumbling routines in which Nowadays' head constantly reappeared between New Guise's legs, so that all gestures towards "it" designated both members; the actual beheading was the culmination of a sword dance in which, as swords were drawn from the Nut, or hexagon of interlocking swords, placed around Nowadays' neck, both Nowadays and New Guise fell to the ground, only to arise and announce themselves cured.[23]

The action is then halted while the folk players directly involve the audience a second time, taking up a collection before they will allow the entrance of a spectacular masked devil (459-61). When the audience has paid all they will, Titivillus enters, monstrous in appearance and evil in intent. He sends the vices off to steal horses and other booty, slips a board under Mankind's sacking (534) so that the "ground" is too hard to work, interrupts Mankind's prayer by drawing attention to his full bladder (560), persuades Mankind that Mercy is hanged for a horse thief and finally, when the vices return, entices Mankind to swear to a life of sin. The folk play, comic and demonic, its roots in pagan topsy-turveydom, has, it would appear, usurped (or reclaimed) the stage from "Christian" forms.

But at this point Mercy returns, and he is changed. His opening lines dispense with form and admit to weakness:

> My mind is dispersed, my body trembleth as the aspen leaf.
> The tears should trickle down by my cheeks, were it not for your
> reverence. (734-35)

Only the presence of the audience keeps him from weeping for the suffering of men, and that only briefly. By the time he leaves in search of Mankind, he has abandoned restraint: "With weeping tears by night

22. Cf. ibid., pp. 50-57, 107-11, 129-31.

23. *Mankind,* directed by Max Harris, Cambridge, June 1969.

and day I will go and never cease" (769). This is a Mercy and a priest no longer speaking conventionally and from a distance to human inconstancy but moved to tears of compassion by it. He recalls the sacrifice of Christ ("Every drop of his blood was shed to purge thine iniquity" [745]) and prays that divine "mercy" towards man should "exceed justice" (758). Mercy will not fail, but thus far the human priest whose costume Mercy wears has failed and in realizing this he has grown. Gone is the self-confidence of the opening sermon; in its stead is a genuine compassion for human weakness.

The audience should have changed too. Just as the Cornish audience was made to share the blame for Christ's death by laughing at the torturer and the blacksmith's wife, so the audience here have shared Mankind's guilt by singing ribald songs with the vices, paying for the appearance of a horrifying devil and laughing at the mockery of Mercy and the downfall of Mankind. Now, if the play has been staged well, what at first seemed innocent mockery of a pompous ecclesiastic has become a rather sordid underworld triumph and the audience will both be conscious of their own fault and ready for relief. When Mercy reappears weeping, the audience should both be delighted by and ready to embrace his fresh compassion.

Mankind too has changed, his self-righteousness dissolved. When Mercy finds him, about to hang himself in despair at the vices' instigation, Mankind cannot believe that God could still be gracious:

> What, ask mercy yet once again? Alas, it were a vile petition,
> Ever to offend and ever to ask mercy, it is a puerility.
> . . . I am not worthy to have mercy by no possibility.
> . . . The equal justice of God will not permit such a sinful
> wretch
> To be revived and restored again; it were impossible.
>
> (819-22, 31-32)

But Mankind is finally convinced that divine justice follows the promptings of divine mercy and, though Mercy unfortunately lapses briefly again into homiletic style, the play ends with Mankind and Mercy reunited and the latter extending God's mercy in blessing to the audience. Neither sermon nor Adam play, on the one hand, nor folk play, on the other, has finally triumphed; rather, if the play as a whole is viewed in retrospect, a skillfully contrived mixed style, in which the reality of fallen human being has been met not with fastidious rejection but with compassion, has held the stage throughout. Both style and stance are merciful to man.

The Cocktail Party

In the first half of this century there was something of a self-conscious revival of "Christian" drama, spearheaded by the work of Paul Claudel in France and T. S. Eliot and Christopher Fry in England. The present context may be the best place to offer a brief assessment of this phenomenon. For, though none of these playwrights viewed himself as bound by the strict neo-classical separation of tragedy and comedy, yet each in some measure avoided the mixed style of rough and holy: their work, even when comic, is always polite. It is worth asking whether this formal restraint limits the extent to which the plays can be fully "Christian" drama.

Eliot's *The Cocktail Party* can serve as a test case. A "comedy" and the most popular of Eliot's plays when first performed, it explores the difficulty of working out one's salvation "with diligence"[24] in the genteel but alienated world of contemporary upper middle-class England, while the "gods" are at work in one to will and to do their good pleasure. Certain aspects of the play point towards "holiness": the blank verse; the loose grounding in the mythic structure of Euripides' *Alcestis;* the occasional biblical phraseology; the "triumphant" martyrdom of Celia Copplestone; and the "guardians" who, led by Harcourt-Reilly/Heracles, are somehow both human and demonic, eccentric mortals and guardian spirits, conspiratorial agents of a mysterious providence. Other aspects ground the play firmly in the "everyday life" of the characters: reference to such mundane problems as being "locked in the lavatory" and failing "to put the cap on a tube of tooth-paste" correctly;[25] the finely observed bickering of Edward and Lavinia at the close of Act One; and the pervasive background, in Acts One and Three, of eating and drinking. But it is not a "rough" life. Even the drinking song of

24. T. S. Eliot, *The Cocktail Party* (London: Faber & Faber, 1958) pp. 128, 145.
25. Ibid., pp. 142, 17, 101.

One-Eyed Riley, though sudden, is discreet. Eliot acknowledged that his intention had been "to produce characters whose drawingroom behaviour was generally correct."[26]

Correct behavior, for Eliot as for Corneille, was a guard against chaos. Harcourt-Reilly offers Celia two forms of "treatment" for her desperate sense of loneliness and failure amidst the polished surfaces of polite society. The first, successfully prescribed for Edward and Lavinia, entails reconciliation with the protective armor of those surfaces, the penetration of which is always "bad form":

> If that is what you wish,
> I can reconcile you to the human condition,
> The condition to which some who have gone as far as you
> Have succeeded in returning. They may remember
> The vision they have had, but they cease to regret it,
> Maintain themselves by the common routine,
> Learn to avoid excessive expectation,
> Become tolerant of themselves and others,
> Giving and taking, in the usual actions
> What there is to give and take. They do not repine;
> Are contented with the morning that separates
> And with the evening that brings together
> For casual talk before the fire
> Two people who know they do not understand each other,
> Breeding children whom they do not understand
> And who will never understand them.

When Celia asks, in dismay, "Is that the best life?," Harcourt-Reilly responds, "It is a good life. . . ./ In a world of lunacy,/ violence, stupidity, greed . . . it is a good life." Celia, however, chooses the higher "way of illumination," "by which the human is/ Transhumanised." She joins "a very austere" nursing order, under whose auspices she is martyred in a tropical jungle, "crucified/ Very near an ant-hill." Though painful, it is, in Harcourt-Reilly's view, both a "triumphant" and "happy death."[27]

There may be practical wisdom in the first way and mystical wisdom in the second, but neither, as Eliot describes them, displays the

26. Quoted in P. Ackroyd, *T. S. Eliot* (New York: Simon & Schuster, 1984) p. 294.
27. Eliot, op. cit., pp. 135, 138-39, 147, 172-74, 179-81.

wisdom of the Incarnation. Celia's choice may be intended to imitate Christ, since it places her amidst the extremes of human suffering, ministering to the minds and bodies of the sick; and, like Christ, she will "not leave the dying natives" and so is crucified. But her choice entails no affirmation of human life. The austerity of her order may be read as a denial of the ordinary joys of human life; and there is no marriage at Cana, no comic upending of the tables of hypocrisy, no hearty laughter in Eliot's description of her missionary service.

The Cocktail Party, it would seem, represents a certain strand of Christian thought that advocates resignation and heroic suffering. This is not entirely without warrant: the biblical writers at times commend patient endurance and self-sacrifice. But they also condemn asceticism (1 Tim. 4:1-5) and fastidiousness (Col. 2:20-23) and testify to an incarnate Word who is both serious and comic, holy and rough. This nuance in the divine Word Eliot seems not to have heard. And, if one may generalize, a weakness not merely in style but in stance of the "Christian" drama of Eliot, Fry and Claudel, has been just this failure to follow the lead of the popular medieval tradition in speaking in an unrestrainedly mixed style. The more refined style, with its conscious savor of classicism, carries with it, if Auerbach is right, a recoil from the broad and muddy world embraced in the gospel.

Chapter 7 Seen and Unseen

Peter Brook has called the Holy Theatre "The Theatre of the Invisible-Made-Visible." Whether it take the form of "gods" flying in from Africa to possess the Haitian dancer or of "the abstract notion of mercy" sliding down the "voodoo pole" of Isabella's silence to become "concrete" in the prolonged moment of her hesitation, "the notion that the stage is a place where the invisible can appear has a deep hold on our thoughts."[1] This should not surprise us. We are, after all, exploring the relationship between the theater and the Christian doctrine of the invisible Word become visible flesh. But it may also disturb us. For it is one thing to suggest that God chose a "theatrical" mode of self-revelation and quite another to propose that human art may conjure up an incarnation in the theater. But Brook is at least bold in his conviction that, while the theater must ground itself in the abrasive surfaces of everyday life, it must also brace itself to reckon with the mysteries of the unseen. The ways in which it has taken up the latter challenge form the substance of this chapter.

Imitating the Unseen

In John Bale's *A Comedy Concerning Three Laws,* written at the height of the English Reformation, God the Father strode on, fully corporeal,

1. Brook, op. cit., pp. 38, 57-58, 81.

and announced, "I am Deus Pater, a substance invisible."[2] By contrast, in John Barton's 1974 production of Marlowe's *Doctor Faustus,* the good and evil angels were represented by "a black voodoo doll and a white toy angel" which the actor playing Faustus "manipulated like glove puppets, speaking their lines as well as his own."[3] What these devices have in common is that they imitate the unseen in visible symbols. The verb is important: they imitate (or denote) but do not claim to embody invisible realities.

Where they differ is in their perception of the nature of the unseen and therefore in the symbols that they use. The one conceives of the unseen in supernatural terms, the other in psychological terms. For Bale, as for the medieval dramatists from whom he inherited the convention, a visible human actor was an appropriate dramatic sign for the invisible God. Though one was infinite spirit and the other finite soul and body, Christian tradition declared that God had made man "in his own image" (Gen. 1:27) and had himself been "born in the likeness of men" (Phil. 2:7). Scriptural precedent sanctioned mimetic sign.

The same held true for the representation of angels and demons. The fifteenth-century author of *Dives et Pauper* explained why, in pictorial art, angels were "painted in likeness of young men since they be spirits and have no bodies":

> There may no painter paint a spirit in his kind, and therefore, to the better representation, they be painted in the likeness of a man, which in soul is most according to angel's kind.[4]

There was scriptural precedent here too: in Old and New Testament alike angels appear as "men" (Gen. 18:2; 19:1; Lk. 24:4; Acts 1:10; Heb. 13:2). If angels appeared as men, men could in play appear as angels. And, since demons were fallen angels, then fallen men, their humanity distorted "in the most horrible manner" by mask and costume,[5] were considered their most apt dramatic image.

2. *The Dramatic Writings of John Bale,* ed. J. S. Farmer (London: Early English Drama Society, 1907) p. 4.

3. A. Riddell, "Edinburgh Shock," *Sunday Telegraph,* 1 September 1974, p. 14.

4. Quoted in Kolve, op. cit., p. 30. I have modernized both spelling and punctuation.

5. "here enteryth Satan in to *þe place in* þe most orryble wyse": *Ludus Coventriae,* ed. K. S. Block, EETS, ES 120 (London: Oxford University Press, 1922) p. 287.

For many modern directors and audiences, however, supernatural concepts are better "demythologized" and old symbols replaced by new. The unseen world resides not in the heavenly realms but in the human conscience. The decision to represent Faustus' angels not as independent spirits but as extensions of himself and to do so by means of glove puppets and not human actors was a deft adaptation of Marlowe's imagery to a modern, psychologically oriented sensibility.

To transpose supernatural imagery into a psychological key may be legitimate theatrical experiment. However, when it becomes an automatic mode of reading texts from a prior culture, it can blind us to the vision of the unseen proposed by those texts. Before we opt, therefore, for an exclusively psychological approach to the "Theatre of the Invisible-Made-Visible," we should first do justice to the medieval understanding and "playing" of unseen conflict.

A case in point is the fifteenth-century morality play, *The Castle of Perseverance.* The centerpiece of the play is a siege of the Castle, to which penitent Mankind has fled and where he is defended by seven virtues. The attack is mounted by the armies of the World, the Flesh and the Devil, consisting in part of seven matching vices. An early twentieth-century critic, whose lead has been followed by most subsequent scholarship, wrote that "the conflict" of the play is a psychological one, a struggle "between man's good and evil inclinations":

> The subjective forces that in reality belong to man himself in the most personal sense were transformed by the poet into visible, external forces. . . . The motives and impulses of man's own heart were taken from him and, clothed in flesh and blood, given him again for companions.[6]

But the vices are described in the text as "devils" and the virtues are defined with reference to the person and work of Christ. The question to bear in mind, therefore, as we imagine the staging of this rough and holy siege, is whether the action to which it refers and which in some sense it "makes visible" is hidden entirely within the human soul or whether it also embraces a supernatural conflict that impinges on humanity from without.

6. E. N. S. Thompson, "The English Moral Plays," *Transactions of the Connecticut Academy of Arts and Sciences,* XIV (March 1910) p. 315.

The castle stands at the center of the outdoor arena, its canvas sides painted to look like stone walls (2042), "stronger than any in France" and "full of virtue and grace" (1553-56).[7] But, from their respective scaffolds on the circumference of the arena, the armies of the World, the Flesh and the Devil march against the castle, trumpets (1898) and bagpipes (2198) blaring and banners flapping in the breeze. They are armed to the teeth with firearms, lances, bows, stones, shields and other weapons. Flesh is on horseback (1940), equipped "with arms from top to toe" (1985). Lechery carries hot coals (2291), Gluttony fire and kindling (1961-68, 2252-53). The Devil has "gunpowder burning in pipes in his hands and in his ears and in his arse."[8] The vices are on several occasions described as "fiends," "devils" and, collectively, "these seven devils" (894-96, 1338, 1979, 2959, 2447) and are no doubt dressed accordingly.

The Devil's army first assaults the castle. Firing bows and hurling stones and firecrackers, Pride, Anger and Envy try to mount the walls of the castle with scaling-ladders. The corresponding virtues, Humility, Patience and Charity, defend themselves with roses (2211, 2222) representing Christ. Anger complains:

> I am all beaten black and blue
> With a rose that on rood was rent. (2219-20)

The virtues are further identified with Christ by Humility's banner, portraying "this meek king" who "alighted with meekness in Mary" and who "was crucified on Calvary" (2083-89), and by the observation that Patience and Charity were best exemplified in him (2125-36, 2173-80).

Flesh's army then takes up the attack. Gluttony and Lechery perhaps try to set fire to the castle. Sloth, armed with a spade, tries to drain the moat of grace that surrounds it (2325-31). But Abstinence wields the Bread of Christ, telling Gluttony she will quench his fire

> With bread that brought us out of hell,
> And on the cross suffered pain:
> I mean the sacrament. (2267-69)

7. *The Macro Plays,* pp. 1-111. I have modernized spelling and occasionally vocabulary in quoting from this play.

8. *The Macro Plays,* p. 1 and frontispiece.

Chastity is armed with water (2383-90), representing both Christ and the Virgin Mary (2302-16) and with which she drenches Lechery (2388). Industry strikes Sloth with a rosary representing prayer (2362); Sloth moans afterwards that his skull is broken and he needs water with which to bathe his aching testicles (2396-2404).

By now six vices have been repulsed; only Covetousness remains. To Generosity's dismay, Covetousness resorts not to direct assault but to the sweet enticements of wealth and property, and by these means Mankind, now an "old man" (2501), is induced to leave the castle voluntarily. Like *Mankind,* however, the play ends with the triumph of divine mercy. In the concluding debate of the Four Daughters of God, following Mankind's death, Mercy reminds her sister Righteousness:

> . . . we were made friends dear
> When the Jews proffered Christ vinegar and gall
> On the Good Friday.
> God granted that remission,
> Mercy, and absolution,
> Through virtue of his passion,
> To no man should be said nay. . . .
> For the least drop of blood
> That God bled on rood
> It had been satisfaction good
> For all mankind's work. (3135-50)

Though Righteousness demurs, God rules in favor of Mercy and instructs his daughters to retrieve Mankind at once from "yon fiend":

> Bring him to me!
> And set him here by my knee,
> In heaven to be,
> In bliss with games and glee. (3577-81)

To read *The Castle of Perseverance* as if the entire drama took place within the human soul is to miss the dual dimension of the Christian tradition of psychomachia, in which the vices represent both human sin and supernatural demons in the service of Satan, and the virtues are at once attributes of Christ and, as the fruit of Christ's work, man's better impulses.[9] As Rosemond Tuve reminds us concerning a similar dual reference in Spenser, we must

> "read" the one [external, supernatural] image so that everything in it means the second inner image as well. . . . It is impressive that all Spenser's readers do this transmuting, and universally stage the action of the *Faerie Queene* within the human heart; the battle perhaps is keeping the poem at least double . . . and not settling for a dwindled *gostly* [psychological] half.[10]

This "double" reading of moral conflict is deeply rooted in the Christian tradition. The apostle Paul warned the Ephesians that they were fighting not only "against flesh and blood" but against the Devil and all "the spiritual hosts of wickedness in the heavenly places" (Eph. 6:12). Eusebius, writing of "wars . . . waged for the very peace of the soul," credited "athletes of piety" with "trophies won from demons, and victories against unseen adversaries"; and Gregory the Great described the vices as "evil spirits," attacking "the soldier of God," who defends himself, "relying on the aid of grace from above." Morton Bloomfield, in his detailed history of the subject, properly concludes that "the Sins were from their earliest appearance in Christian thought considered concrete devils or demons."[11]

The virtues, on the other hand, were understood to be attributes of Christ poured out on his body the Church in the form of seven spiritual gifts. Gregory wrote that "our Redeemer, . . . grieved that we were held captive by these seven sins . . . , came to the spiritual battle of our liberation, full of the spirit of sevenfold grace." Following Ambrose, he identified "the seven virtues of the Holy Spirit" with the seven gifts of the Spirit, promised by Isaiah (11:2-3 LXX), realized in Christ, and then granted to his body the Church "as special aids to the Christian in his

9. For a fuller discussion of what follows, see Max Harris, "Flesh and Spirits: the Battle between Virtues and Vices in Medieval Drama Reassessed," *Medium Aevum,* LVII, 1 (1988) pp. 56-64.

10. R. Tuve, *Allegorical Imagery* (Princeton: Princeton University Press, 1966) p. 112.

11. Eusebius, *The Ecclesiastical History,* trans. K. Lake and J. E. L. Oulton, Loeb Classical Library (Cambridge: Harvard University Press, 1926-32), I, p. 406; Gregory the Great, *Morals on the Book of Job,* trans. Rev. J. Bliss (Oxford: Parker, 1844-50), III, pp. 483-84; M. W. Bloomfield, *The Seven Deadly Sins* (Michigan: Michigan State College Press, 1952) p. 34.

war against evil."[12] This identification of spiritual gifts and virtues remained popular throughout the Middle Ages and, as Rosemond Tuve has concluded,

> affected all treatments of virtues so persistently that it must be considered by anyone who wishes to understand such discussions, literary or theological, at least as late as the sixteenth and seventeenth centuries.[13]

What is portrayed in *The Castle of Perseverance,* therefore, is not just a psychological struggle. It is Christ, and not man alone, who battles with the vices. And it is Satan and his minions, and not man alone, who resists. This battle is waged in and for each individual soul and, over the course of history, for the human race in its entirety. The play in fact displays the same beginning, middle and end as the Corpus Christi plays: the fall of man in response to demonic temptation and his own rebellion; Christ's victory over sin on the cross, making possible a similar victory in the lives of individual Christians, both of these represented by the victory of the virtues over the vices on behalf of Mankind; and the final deliverance of redeemed mankind to peace in heaven. The invisible history of the race and of each individual, taking place at once in the heavens and in the soul, is imitated in a single dramatic action.

Expressing the Unseen

It is imitated (or denoted), but it is not embodied. The actors playing the vices are dressed like demons but are not possessed; those playing the virtues represent Christ but are not a theophany. We can, however, move a step closer to the kind of "incarnational" theater that Brook has in mind if, for the time being, we limit ourselves to the psychological dimension. For it is easier to accept that the theater can give tangible expression to hidden emotions than it is to grant that gods can materialize on stage.

12. Gregory, op. cit., III, p. 490 and I, pp. 52-53; Ambrose, *De Sacramentis,* in *Patrologia Latina,* ed. J.-P. Migne (Paris: Gamier, 1844-63) XVI, col. 434; P. F. Mulhern, "Holy Spirit, Gifts of," *The New Catholic Encyclopedia.*

13. Tuve, op. cit., p. 89; cf. Bloomfield, op. cit., pp. 77, 89, 124, 177.

We can begin with a moment from Racine's *Phèdre,* in which every element of the theatrical language combines to give startling expression to the character's inner life. When Phèdre first enters, she staggers under the weight of her regalia. Demanding rest, she confesses to a burden of emotion as well as ornament. Then, "in a momentous gesture of submission," "she sits down" (I, iii). "Elsewhere in Racine and in neoclassical drama," George Steiner observes, "tragic personages do not sit down. . . . When Phèdre sits . . . she lets slip the reins of reason."[14] For a moment, angrily, she tries to sustain the pretence that her exhaustion is caused only by the weight of jewelry and coiffure:

> Tear off these gross, official rings, undo
> these royal veils. They drag me to the ground.
> Why have you frilled me, laced me, crowned me, and wound
> my hair in turrets? All your skill torments
> and chokes me. I am crushed by ornaments.
> Everything hurts me, and drags me to my knees![15]

But at last the vehemence of her language and the persistence of her nurse betrays her. Reluctantly she confesses her passion for Hippolytus.

The scene's power derives from the precise correspondence between visual data, spoken word and revealed emotion. What we see initially is a queen literally weighed down by her desire to maintain appearances, the external burden of pomp and finery an emblem of her hidden struggle to abide by a morality to which she subscribes but which she can barely sustain. When she sits, she signals her involuntary surrender. Her rings and veils are removed, her hair loosed and her illicit passion painfully declared. Visual image and spoken word conspire to express, with an intensity that words alone could not, otherwise "invisible" inner torment.

What Racine did for his characters' conscious but unexpressed emotions, many a playwright at the end of the nineteenth century be-

14. Steiner, op. cit., p. 88.

15. Racine, *Phaedra,* trans. R. Lowell, in E. Bentley (ed.), *The Classic Theatre,* 4 vols. (Garden City, New York: Doubleday Anchor, 1958-61) IV, p. 136. Lowell's "version" of Racine's play is often more powerful than any of the more strict translations and I have quoted it here for that reason.

gan to attempt for his own newly fashionable unconscious mind. The combination of impressions made at any given moment by the words and action, costume and decor, music and lighting were supposed to form a composite sensory image of an invisible psychological state. While, at one level, it was the characters' inner life that was being given concrete expression, it was also believed that the characters were projections of the poet's psyche and that the multitude of simultaneous and consecutive sensory impressions that constituted the drama were therefore a tangible expression of the poet's own unconscious mind. What had been hidden even from him was made visible in the act of writing and performance.

Maeterlinck's *Pélléas and Mélisande* serves as a good example of this Symbolist aesthetic. On the level of plot, it is a fairy tale of fated love in a mythical kingdom: a royal prince, Golaud, meets a mysterious young girl, Mélisande, by a forest spring and marries her; back at the castle, Mélisande falls in love with Golaud's brother, Pélléas; Golaud, smitten with jealousy, kills the lovers.

In one of the best-known scenes, Golaud discovers Pélléas fondling and kissing Mélisande's long, unbound hair. Immediately he leads his brother into the dank vaults beneath the castle (III, iii). It is a place of eery danger, of stagnant water poisoning the castle air and of "strange lizards" scampering in and out of cracks, of darkness, "the smell of death" and sudden drops into unplumbed gulfs. Golaud warns Pélléas to "take care," to walk in the light of his lantern and to heed his directions. At one point Pélléas nearly slips into an abyss, but at the last moment Golaud "seizes him by the arm": "For God's sake! . . . Don't you see? – One step more, and you'd have been in the gulf! . . ." Pélléas protests, "But I didn't see it! . . . The lantern no longer lighted me . . . ," and Golaud admits, "I made a false step . . . but if I hadn't held you by the arm . . ."[16]

As Christopher Innes has observed, "It is immediately clear that this is a descent into the abysses of the subconscious mind."[17] The scene expresses the unacknowledged strength of Golaud's jealousy. At the conscious level, he is still describing his younger brother's flirta-

16. M. Maeterlinck, *Théâtre* (Brussels: Lacomblez, 1912) II, pp. 4-113. My translation.

17. C. Innes, *Holy Theatre* (Cambridge: Cambridge University Press, 1981) p. 19.

tion with Mélisande as "child's play" (III, iv). But at the subconscious level, he is deeply angry, ready to kill Pélléas and barely holding back. The imagery, visual and spoken, of the scene in the vaults gives concrete expression to these dangerous but as yet repressed emotions.

But the scene captures more than just the particular psyche of Golaud. Maeterlinck has forged a powerful image of the repressive mind in general, perched precariously, for all its defensive walls and locked doors, on top of the terrifying and unstable foundations of an unexplored subconscious. Golaud's comment that "there are hidden workings here that no one suspects, and the whole castle will be engulfed one of these nights, if we do not take heed," is intended as a warning not only to his own conscious self but to all who rely too much on "rational" self-control.

Maeterlinck's conception of his own mode of composition reflects this distrust of rational control. Recalling "Emerson's carpenter," who, when he hews a beam, places it at his feet so that "the universe," in the form of gravity, "seconds and multiplies the least movement of his muscles," he argues that "it is just so with the poet":

> His power is greater or less, not because of his own doing, but . . . by the mysterious eternal order and the occult forces of things. He should place himself in an attitude where eternity may bear up his words, and every notion of his mind be seconded and multiplied by the gravitation of the one and eternal mind. The poet, it seems to me, ought to be passive towards symbolism, and the purest kind is perhaps that which makes itself felt in spite of him and even contrary to his intention.[18]

Applied to *Pélléas and Mélisande,* this would mean that not only the particular images of the play, but the way in which they are arranged and juxtaposed, as well as the characters and the progression of their moods and interactions, sprung not from Maeterlinck's conscious invention but from the yielding of his unconscious mind to the "gravitational pull" of "the one and eternal mind." In other words, what is projected on stage is not finally the psyche of the characters nor even of the author but of the universe. The play descends into Golaud's sub-

18. Quoted in the Introduction to *Pélléas and Mélisande,* trans. E. Winslow (New York: Crowell, 1894) pp. 11-12.

conscious and finds itself expressing, through the medium of the poet, the universal mind.

This should not surprise anyone familiar with the histories of nineteenth-century philosophy and psychology: the more one delves into the narrow confines of the nineteenth-century "mind," the more the individual psyche seems to expand unexpectedly into a universal mind. The very language of psychiatry at the time was ambiguous. For, according to historians of the science, "the term 'unconscious' was used by several authors as an alternative for the 'universal will' of the natural philosophers."[19] K. G. Carus was one who, in his book *Psyche* (1846), used the term "unconscious" in this way. Another was K. E. von Hartmann, "a philosopher much influenced by Schopenhauer, [who] contributed to this semantic shift from 'will' to 'unconscious mind' in his *Philosophy of the Unconscious* (1869)."[20] For these men, the individual "unconscious" was a particular expression of the universal "unconscious," just as, for Schopenhauer, the individual act of volition had been a particular manifestation of the universal will.

Thus when Freud in 1895 discovered that, "by asking his patients to abandon conscious control over their ideas and to say whatever came into their minds," he could by such "free association" learn much about his patients' "unconscious minds," there was inherent in the terms a certain ambiguity. This was enhanced when in 1900 he published *The Interpretation of Dreams,* in which he suggested that dreams, properly interpreted, were also "a royal road to the unconscious."[21] For dreams had long been regarded by the Romantics and their followers as a means by which the universal "world spirit" revealed itself. Likewise Jung's concept of the "collective unconscious," a common mythology of archetypal symbols used by dreamers, worshippers and artists to express truths beyond the reach of the conscious mind, again provided a universal of which the "personal unconscious" was a particular expression.[22]

Buoyed up by notions such as these, artists like Maeterlinck and, later, the Dadaists and Surrealists believed that by yielding themselves

19. F. G. Alexander and S. T. Selesnick, *The History of Psychiatry* (New York: Harper & Row, 1966) p. 169.

20. Ibid., pp. 145, 170. Cf. the discussion of Carus in B. Knapp, *Maurice Maeterlinck* (Boston: Twayne, 1975) pp. 141-42.

21. Alexander and Selesnick, op. cit., pp. 194-95.

22. Ibid., p. 246.

to an ambiguous "unconscious" they could not merely imitate but actually express the invisible on stage. And since it was not merely, as in *Phèdre,* the fictional invisible of a character's emotions that was being expressed, but the actual invisible of the author's unconscious mind and, if we are to believe the claims, the unseen vibrations of the universal mind, we have come very close to the concept of an "incarnational" theater advocated by Brook. Not gods, to be sure, but the universal mind was taking flesh on stage.

Summoning the Unseen

Artaud invoked the gods. If there is any single figure who drew together the several strands of "holy" theater apparent at the beginning of this century, shocked them free of any lingering ethereality and passed them on fused and vibrant to the modern theater, it is Antonin Artaud. But Artaud's life also serves notice of the proximity of holy theater to occult ritual and the dangers of an indiscriminate evocation of the unseen.

In 1926 in Paris Artaud founded the Théâtre Alfred Jarry. The manifestoes issued to announce its opening declare that, "amid the confusion, the absence, the distortion of all human values, in this agonizing uncertainty in which we live," to look on the theater as an "amusement" is derisory. To re-establish "an absolutely pure theatre," an audience must be found, willing to "join forces" with the Théâtre Alfred Jarry in a "mystical experiment," in which a hidden world, a "world tangential to objective reality," may be revealed. In such a theater, "all that is obscure, hidden, and unrevealed in the mind will be manifested in a kind of material, objective projection," which will constitute "an authentic performance of magic." The formal means to this ambitious end were as yet ill defined. Artaud noted only that the "picturesque" settings of contemporary Naturalism were a dead end and that "*mise en scène* properly speaking . . . must be regarded as the visible signs of an invisible language."[23]

Artaud found his theatrical "signs" when, in 1931, he saw a troupe of Balinese dancers perform in Paris. It was, he wrote, "the most beautiful manifestation of pure theatre it has been our privilege to see." What struck him especially was this ritual theater's "new physical language,

23. Artaud, *Selected Writings,* pp. 155-62.

based upon signs and no longer upon words." "Geometric robes . . . , displacing the axis of the human figure," "muscular facial expressions, applied to the features like masks," and inhuman noises, "syncopated modulations formed at the back of the throat, . . . musical phrases that break off short, . . . sounds of hollow drums, . . . robot squeakings," all contributed to a "systematic depersonalization" of the dancers, rendering them "veritable living, moving hieroglyphs."

Through these "spiritual signs" there was made manifest an invisible "conflict of spiritual states." The body of the dancer, at times "stiffened by the tide of cosmic forces which besiege it," became a vehicle of "miraculous revelation," whose meaning "strikes us only intuitively but with enough violence to make useless any translation into logical discursive language." Nor was the audience exempt from such possession. The concentrated goal of the performance, to which it directed its "efficacious means," was to serve as "an exorcism to make our demons FLOW." Presiding over this material disclosure of cosmic forces was

> a director who has become a kind of manager of magic, a master of sacred ceremonies. And the material on which he works, the themes which he brings to throbbing life are derived not from him but from the gods. . . . What he sets in motion is the MANIFESTED.[24]

Artaud's practical work in the theater, though not extensive, and his theoretical essays, published in *The Theater and Its Double,* have proved highly influential. One need only recall Brook's production of *Orghast,* with its hieratic action, arcane language and "possessed" cast, "creating a circle" with the audience "in which the impulse can go round," or the work of such recent directors as Jerzy Grotowski, Jerome Savary and Luca Ronconi, to realize how much.

But Artaud himself finally abandoned "play" in search of authentic ritual. In 1936 he left France to spend six months among the Tarahumara Indians in the mountains of northern Mexico. There he watched the dance of the *matachines,* for which a bull was sacrificed, its flesh eaten raw and its warm blood drunk by dancers and spectators alike. Incantations accompanied the dance, as "a secret summons to I know not what dark forces, what presences from *the beyond.*" Likewise

24. Artaud, *The Theater and Its Double,* pp. 53-67.

he watched peyote dancers achieve a trance state in which they followed "the secret commands issued to them by the Peyote." Artaud himself partook of the peyote and was convinced he had made contact, under its influence, with the Tarahumara god Ciguri.

On another occasion, when he was "bewitched," Artaud summoned "sorcerers" to heal him. He describes their arrival, supporting themselves on huge staffs and bent under the weight of their magical apparatus. Fires were lit and dancing began. Two young goats had been killed, "and now I saw, on a branchless tree trunk that had also been carved in the shape of a cross, the lungs and hearts of the animals trembling in the night wind." A circle was staked out, a circle so evil "that birds who stray into this circle fall, and . . . pregnant women feel their embryos rot inside them." At sunset a sorcerer entered the circle, "moving forward deliberately into evil, immersing himself in it with a kind of terrible courage." The dance continued all night until, shortly before dawn, Artaud shared peyote with the dancers and was then led towards the circle. There "strange words" were uttered over him while he was sprinkled with water. With this the "cure" was ended.[25]

After a subsequent voyage to Ireland, again in search of authentic magic, Artaud was arrested and confined to an asylum. He was to spend most of the rest of his life in such institutions. The exact nature of Artaud's madness is still under dispute but, in view of his long-standing evocation of "dark forces," we should not take lightly his own claim that "hordes of demons . . . afflict me night and day."[26] However one conceptualizes the demonic, Artaud stands as a warning that the "dark forces," within or without the human psyche, may not always be glove puppets under our control and that to enter the circle of "holy" theater unwarily is a hazardous step.

"The Mystery, Which Is Christ in You"

Both *The Castle of Perseverance* and Artaud's vision of authentic ritual presume the reality of an unseen world of spirits whose activity im-

25. Artaud, *The Peyote Dance,* trans. H. Weaver (New York: Farrar, Strauss & Giroux, 1976) pp. 64-69, 20-36.

26. Artaud, *Selected Writings,* p. 423.

pinges upon and affects the unseen workings of the human mind. Both seek to present the hidden conflicts of these dual realms in visible signs. Why, then, should one be content to imitate the unseen, never venturing invocation, and the other boldly summon the unseen, scorning all but "magical mimesis"?

The difference may lie in the centrality of Christ in the medieval playwright's artistic vision. For in *The Castle of Perseverance* the dramatized battle is not finally between opposing spirits but between Christ and the forces of darkness. The virtues are at once attributes of Christ, triumphing over Satan in the history of salvation, and gifts of the Spirit of Christ, resisting sin within the human soul. This twofold presence of "God with us," being and acting in and for mankind in Christ, renders the evocation of lesser spirits a paltry alternative. Such at least is the argument of the Letter to the Colossians.

There the writer addresses a church tempted to worship angels and other "elemental spirits of the universe" and to boast of "visions" arising from such worship (Col. 2:8, 18, 20). That "the worship of angels" was not merely an innocent fascination with spiritual ministers of Christ, but something much more akin to Artaud's "magic," is made likely not only by its explicit condemnation in the letter but by Irenaeus' juxtaposition, in *Against Heresies,* of "angelic invocations" and "incantations, or . . . any other wicked curious art."[27] In the view of the writer to the Colossians, such "invocations" are to be avoided not because they may not "work" or, though he no doubt believed this, because there is a danger in the indiscriminate evocation of "angels" that one may summon less friendly spirits, but finally because they offer so much less than the Christian already has in Christ.

Christ, he writes, is the Lord of all creation. "All things were created . . . in him . . . [and] through him and for him," including everything "in heaven and on earth, visible and invisible" and, most notably in this context, whatever hierarchies of angels the Colossians may be tempted to invoke, "whether thrones or dominions or principalities or powers." Christ is "before all things," without exception, "and in him all things hold together." Not only is he, as the recipient and instrument of all creation and its preserver moment by moment, Lord over all things in general. He is also, by virtue of his resurrection as "the

27. Irenaeus, *Against Heresies,* II, xxxii, 5.

first-born from the dead," head in particular of the Church, which is described in a now familiar but once astounding image of intimacy as his "body." Why then invoke angels when one has access to Christ, who is "in everything . . . pre-eminent" (1:16-18)?

Perhaps the Colossians were being tempted by an incipient Gnosticism and being told that they could approach Christ only through an intermediate hierarchy of angels and other spirits whom they must first invoke and worship.[28] The writer counteracts this suggestion in two stages. First he affirms that "in Christ all the fullness of God was pleased to dwell" (1:19) and that "bodily" (2:9). The doctrine of the Incarnation, understood as the enfleshing of "all the fullness of God" in Christ, stood in stark contrast to the Gnostic conviction that God and matter were for ever separated by vast mutual recoil, the intervening gulf filled only by spiritual beings who, as they came closer to man, were further removed from God.

Secondly, the writer makes the astonishing assertion that this Christ, in whom "the whole fullness of deity dwells bodily," is now "Christ in you" (1:27). This concept occurs often in the Pauline Epistles, the emphasis falling alternately on Christ being in the redeemed (Rom. 8:10, 2 Cor. 13:15) and on the synonymous (cf. Rom. 8:9 and 10) indwelling of the Holy Spirit in the individual Christian (1 Cor. 6:19) and in the Church as a whole (Eph. 2:22). Familiarity may have dulled for some the brilliance of this gospel, but for the Colossians it must have shone clearly against the murky background of Gnostic visions and invocations. If Christ himself lives in the Christian and in the Church, what can possibly be gained by yielding oneself as an instrument or habitation of lesser spirits?

Moreover, the writer to the Colossians, like the author of *The Castle of Perseverance,* proclaims that "this mystery, which is Christ in you" (Col. 1:27) aids the Christian in his own struggle with the forces of sin. Throughout his life and most particularly at the cross, Christ "disarmed" those unseen "principalities and powers" who opposed him, overcoming their temptations and publishing their defeat by leading them, as it were, as prisoners in triumphal procession (2:15).[29] He now

28. J. B. Lightfoot, *Saint Paul's Epistles to the Colossians and to Philemon* (London: Macmillan, 1879) pp. 73-113.

29. My understanding of this verse, which differs from that of the RSV translation, follows Lightfoot, op. cit., pp. 189-92.

wins within the Christian a consequent and similar victory. Christ is "our life" (3:4), living within us and there creating a "new nature" (3:9), freed from "the dominion of darkness" (1:13) and enabled more and more to shed the old sins (3:5-9) and to put on the character traits of Christ (3:12-15). What attraction can there be therefore for the Christian, in whom Christ is crafting godliness, to seek approximation to divinity in the evocation of forces over whom Christ has triumphed and over whom he has given the Christian victory?

Critics have detected "distinct gnostic leanings"[30] in Artaud's work. We should not therefore be surprised to find him embracing an aesthetic implicitly rejected by the Letter to the Colossians. However, our excursion into this epistle does more than shed light on the particular difference between Artaud and *The Castle of Perseverance.* It also provides some limits to the analogy we are exploring between the theater and the Christian doctrine of the Incarnation. In its use of signs that move through time and space and which imitate the world beyond performance, seen and unseen, the theater may well bear a likeness to that sensory mode of divine self-revelation attested in the classic texts of the Christian faith. But, at least for the Christian, the theater will not move beyond likeness to rival, claiming to emulate the Incarnation by summoning spirit or universal will to inhabit its material signs. It will be content to give greater clarity to what is often hidden, whether it be the spiritual and psychological struggle of Mankind in *The Castle of Perseverance* or the turmoil of a queen caught between decorum and desire in *Phèdre,* and in doing so it may often reveal in sudden and startling ways what an audience has never understood before. But the theater will not aspire to speak into flesh the word of the universal mind or to summon from an unseen realm "gods" able "to make our demons FLOW." The proclamation that "all the fullness of God" became flesh once for all in Christ and continues incarnate in the members of his body, the Church, sets limits, for the Christian, to the theatrical evocation of spirits.

30. N. Greene, *Antonin Artaud: Poet Without Words* (New York: Simon & Schuster, 1970) p. 118; cf., in *The Theater and Its Double,* pp. 48-52 especially.

Chapter 8 Conflict and Resolution

We have spoken of the theater's affirmation or distrust of human time and space; of its willingness to celebrate both rough and holy or its fastidious determination to create a play world more decorous than God's; and of its capacity to imitate and its temptation to summon the unseen. And we have suggested that the degree to which a play embraces one or other of these variables reveals in great measure its evaluative stance towards the world outside performance. A final and perhaps most important index of a play's stance has to do with its assessment of conflict and resolution.

For drama, by its nature, addresses the problem of conflict and the hope of resolution. The conflict may be trivial, as it was in the French "well-made plays" of the nineteenth century and as it has been in many a more or less entertaining situation comedy since. It may be a particular instance of utmost seriousness: a conflict between love and duty in Corneille, for example, or between rival claimants to a throne in Shakespeare. Or the dramatist may aspire to the imitation or, as Artaud would have it, "the exteriorization of a kind of essential drama," in which all conflict has its roots and which therefore sheds light on "an infinite perspective of conflicts."[1]

The nature of the resolution too may vary. Mass carnage restores a just peace of sorts at the end of Jacobean tragedy; multiple weddings loose the tangled knots of romance at the close of Shakespearean com-

1. Artaud, *The Theater and Its Double,* p. 50.

edy; damnation and blessing together resolve the Corpus Christi plays. The resolution may be satisfying or deeply disturbing, exuberant or ironic. But, as we shall see, it is in its decision as to the nature of conflict and the means, if any, of resolution that a play most clearly declares its evaluative stance.

King Lear

Karl Barth has written of a "conflict with nothingness," and the phrase may serve as a provisional description of the essential drama which Shakespeare's *King Lear* "makes visible." Though Barth finally and determinedly defines nothingness *(das Nichtige)* in explicitly Christian terms, he is willing initially to speak simply of "an alien factor," of "opposition and resistance" and "chaos," of nothingness as "intrinsically evil, . . . both perverting and perverted," and to recognize that, in the human imagination, nothingness often "assumes the form of a monster which, vested with demonic qualities, inspires fear" and even "respect."[2]

Poor Tom, in *King Lear*, is in the grip of the demonic. "When the foul fiend rages," Tom feeds on the refuse of nature, eating cow-dung and ditch-drowned dog and drinking scum from stagnant pools, announcing his diet to the accompaniment of howling winds and pelting rain. Nature is not kind to Tom and, as far as Tom is concerned, is at once the playground and the ally of demons. It is "the foul fiend" who leads him "through fire and through flame, through ford and whirlpool, o'er bog and quagmire"; it is "the foul fiend Flibbertigibbet" who nightly deforms humanity with squint-eyes and hare-lips, "mildews the white wheat, and hurts the poor creature of the earth." "Demons," writes Barth, "are nothingness in its dynamic, to the extent that it has form and power and movement and activity."[3]

The storm bespeaks the same apparent power of nothingness. Nature is both oppressor and victim. "The to-and-fro conflicting wind and rain," the "sheets of fire" lightening the sky and resounding in "bursts of horrid thunder," drench and terrify human and animal kind

2. Barth, *CD,* 3/3, pp. 359-60, 289, 353-54, 293.
3. Ibid., p. 523.

alike. Even "the lion and belly-pinched" and hungry "wolf" dare not hunt, for, as Kent observes,

> the wrathful skies
> Gallow [frighten] the very wanderers of the dark,
> And make them keep their caves.

For Lear "this dreadful pother o'er our heads" should be the judgement of "the great gods" against "undivulged crimes,/ Unwhipp'd of justice." But by his own account the gods take poor aim: he who claims to be "a man/ More sinn'd against than sinning" is the butt of the storm's wrath, while his ungrateful daughters are secure within the castle (III, ii). And Gloucester, remembering "last night's storm," suspects these "gods" of perverse malice:

> As flies to wanton boys are we to the gods, –
> They kill us for their sport. (IV, i)

The storm, like madness, is a phenomenon not easily explained in moral terms. Yet it serves, within the dramatic economy of the play, as a representative brute fact that, if the sovereign power of nothingness is to be denied, must somehow be accommodated in a character's moral universe. How the turbulence of nature is accommodated determines a character's place in the political conflict of the play, and in this way the political struggle becomes the expression of a broader conflict between widely divergent moral "readings" of man's environment.

The bastard Edmund, for example, approves nature as an opponent of custom and moral restraint. It was "in the lusty stealth of nature" that he was conceived, and he has turned out as well-formed as any "honest madam's issue." Nature, it seems, has not punished but rather commended his father's offense against custom. Why should she not then also aid Edmund's challenge to Edgar's "legitimate" right of inheritance? "Thou, nature, art my goddess," is Edmund's creed; "to thy law/ My services are bound" (I, ii). But Edmund is also ready with artifice to further nature's cause. He delivers his apostrophe to nature holding a letter, proposing parricide, that he has written in his brother's handwriting and which he will shortly, despite feigned reluctance, give to his father. Nature, for Edmund, favors the responsibility of human cunning.

But such a libertine view of nature may in turn be read as an alliance with nothingness. The trial of Gloucester, engineered by Edmund and administered by Cornwall, Goneril and Regan, is in many ways the complement within the castle of the storm that rages without. Possessing power, Gloucester's enemies may dispense with all but "the form of justice" and, like "the gods" of nature, indulge their wrath unchecked (III, vii). Nothingness, however, is a treacherous ally. Just as nature storms at herself, so finally do those who treat her amorality as license for "natural" impulse and appetite. After Cornwall is killed by an offended servant, his widow Regan and her sister Goneril compete for Edmund's sexual favor. In her jealousy, Goneril poisons Regan, and when Edmund is defeated in battle, kills herself. Unchecked, natural "humanity must perforce prey on itself,/ Like monsters of the deep" (IV, ii).

A more traditional, Aristotelian reading of nature is espoused by Lear and Gloucester. Believing, as Lear says, that it is "by all the operation of the orbs" that "we do exist and cease to be" (I, i), they also believe fiercely in a "natural" hierarchy of human relationships whose fixed degrees reflect the order of the spheres. Proper observation of these

> offices of nature, bond of childhood,
> Effects of courtesy, dues of gratitude, (II, iv)

is essential to social harmony. Nature is read as an advocate of custom and stability. Thus Gloucester insists that lack of respect for Lear as father and king is "unnatural" (III, iii) and, when he is tried, protests his captors' disruption of the natural laws of hospitality. Blinded, he calls on Edmund, whom he still trusts, to "enkindle all the sparks of nature/ To quit this horrid act" (III, vi). And Lear, when he is rebuffed by Goneril, calls on the "dear goddess . . . nature" to punish the offense of filial ingratitude with infertility (I, v).

But a mechanistic nature, governed by planetary influence, is by definition deaf to human prayer. And nature's aberrations loom large. Early in the play Gloucester muses on the social effect of planetary abnormality, believing that he discerns a link between "these late eclipses in the sun and moon" and the "discord" that threatens the hierarchical relationships he holds so dear. But it is, says Edmund, "an admirable evasion of whoremaster man," to "make guilty of our disasters the sun, the moon, and the stars: as if we were villains by necessity; fools by heavenly compulsion" (I, ii). In any case, by the time of the storm scene, both Lear and Gloucester have lost their faith in nature. Concluding that nature's pattern is marred, Lear calls on the thunder to end nature's human experiment and shortly afterwards sinks into insanity. Gloucester, unable any longer to refrain from quarrelling with the "great opposeless wills" of the "mighty gods," attempts suicide (IV, vi). Both men have surrendered to a sovereign nothingness.

If there were only Lear and Gloucester to resist the advocates of natural and amoral appetite, the play's political conflict would end quickly in a crushing defeat for the representatives of the old morality. But there is a third group of characters in the play who "read" nature in yet another way. Cordelia, Edgar, Kent and finally Albany also believe in the virtues of loyalty and respect but, unlike Lear and Gloucester, are willing to act decisively in their defense. Combining Edmund's active reading of human responsibility with Lear's and Gloucester's commitment to a morality of natural order, they are fit opponents for Edmund and his kind. Edgar and Cordelia honor their fathers, despite parental ingratitude and senility. Never do they try to rule them, but gently work to heal them of insanity and despair. Kent, though he too can say that "It is the stars,/The stars above us, govern our conditions" (IV, ii), belies that fatalism with his persistent and active loyalty to the king who has peremptorily banished him. Together they work at great cost to themselves to restore political order. They are, to use the language of Karl Barth, "the hero[es] who must suffer and fight and finally conquer this adversary" of nothingness, regarding "the conflict with it" as "the problem of [man's] destiny and decision, his tragedy and courage, his impotence and comparative successes."[4]

It would be wrong, however, to give the impression that the play is merely a conflict of ideologies. A play so rich engages its audience at many levels and our first response is likely to be a fairly simple emotional one. We care for Cordelia because her love for her father, unlike that of Goneril and Regan, is genuine. We dislike Edmund because, unlike Edgar, he is self-centered and cruel. We pity Lear and Gloucester because they are misused, while at the same time we are frustrated by their foolishness. Having engaged our emotions, however, Shakespeare suggests that the features to which we have responded in a particular

4. Ibid., pp. 357-58.

character are linked in some measure to a general mode of reading man and his environment. It is not a morality play, in which there is an identity between character and universal. Nor, however, is it just a conflict of particulars, in which characters represent nothing but themselves.

The apparent climax of the dramatic conflict, both on the level of particular characters in whose fortunes we have become deeply involved and on the level of collision between moral and amoral readings of nature, between hero and "nothingness," is the trial by battle between Edmund and Edgar (V, iii). Text ("Alarums. They fight.") only hints at the drama of this moment in performance. Edmund has entered in triumphal procession at the head of his army, drums beating and colors flying, Lear and Cordelia in the rear as prisoners. But, on Albany's orders, a charge of treason is read against Edmund, to be maintained in trial by battle. A first trumpet sounds to summon any knight who dares to prove the charge. There is silence. A second call also goes unanswered. Then, as the third and final trumpet fades, at last another echoes in the distance. The challenger enters, giving no name, his identity concealed behind his armor. The soldiers of Albany's army form a makeshift tilt-yard, and Edmund and the anonymous knight, weighed down with armor and wielding heavy broadswords, fight.

The audience knows that the challenger is Edgar, the feigned madness of his Poor Tom role exchanged for the anonymity of armor, and suspect that the outcome of the whole play depends on this single combat. The local conflict for sound government hangs in the balance. The legitimate heir fights the bastard usurper. But it is more than a local conflict. Order against disorder, justice against injustice, authority against rebellion, filial love against filial contempt, moral man against natural man: the combat between Edgar and Edmund embraces all these in a single enacted metaphor. Even the battle between Christ and Satan is recalled. In the familiar Harrowing of Hell episode in the Corpus Christi plays, Christ, his deity disguised in human flesh and his cause apparently defeated at the cross, went dressed as a knight into his enemy's camp and at the very gates of hell challenged Satan to single combat in the lists.[5] The audience is being made to invest everything,

5. *The Towneley Plays,* G. England and A. Pollard (eds.), EETS, ES 71 (London: Oxford University Press, 1966) pp. 261, 293-305; cf. Kolve, op. cit., pp. 192-96 and Langland, *Piers Plowman,* XVIII.

even at an archetypal level its own redemption, in the outcome of the fight on stage. To our intense relief, Edgar wins.

If *King Lear* had ended here the resolution proposed would be simple. The audience would be invited to join with Edgar in declaring that "the gods are just," with Albany that "the judgment of the heavens" is sound (V, iii) and, in Christian terms, that Christ's victory over Satan holds. Though society descends at times, like nature, into temporary and stormy disorder, and virtue must go disguised as madness, all is at last righted by the blessing of the gods on human virtue and courage.

But there is a second climax that explodes this too easy resolution. Edmund confesses as he dies that he has ordered Cordelia's execution, and Edgar sends quickly to countermand the order. Albany prays confidently, "The gods defend her!" Immediately, Lear enters howling, "Cordelia dead in his arms." Those watching are reminded of the Last Judgement. Kent asks, "Is this the promised end?"; Edgar, "Or image of that horror?" Albany pleads, in language borrowed from biblical apocalypse, for the relief of dissolution: "Fall, and cease" (cf. Rev. 6:15-16; Hos. 10:8). In both of Shakespeare's sources, Holinshed's *Chronicles* and the old play of *King Leir,* Cordelia lived. Her execution here, an instant before redemption, seems expressly designed to shatter any hope that the "gods," if there be any, are in sympathy with the good.

So does Lear's final insanity. Cordelia had pleaded with the "kind gods" to cure his madness, "this great breach in his abused nature" (IV, vii), and in the careful hands of her physician Lear's health had been restored. "The rack of this rough world," on which he had been stretched so long (V, iii), had, as it were, been relaxed. But only for a moment. With her death, the pressure is suddenly and lethally increased, and he snaps.

Shakespeare added one further touch to suggest that the restoration of order is no more normative than the descent into chaos. With the death of all Lear's children, Albany, as the widower of Lear's eldest daughter, inherits the throne. He promptly resigns it. While Lear still lives, insane, Albany announces:

> For us, we will resign,
> During the life of this old majesty,
> To him our absolute power.

When Lear dies, Albany turns to Kent and Edgar:

> Friends of my soul, you twain
> Rule in this realm, and the gor'd state sustain. (V, iii)

Kent refuses. He must shortly follow his "master" Lear into death; whether by his own hand or not is left unclear. Edgar finally accepts. While we may feel that the crown has finally settled on the wisest head, it is disconcerting, in a play whose terrifying slide into political and moral chaos was initiated by Lear's resignation of his authority, to see his heirs divest themselves in such quick succession of inherited responsibility. This too is Shakespeare's addition to his sources, and leaves the audience not with the confidence of order permanently restored but with the lingering suspicion that the whole cycle of disorder is about to begin again.

For Edgar, like Barth's "hero," is convinced that man "must suffer and fight and finally conquer this adversary" of nothingness. But Barth does not approve of heroes. He adds at once:

> There can be no greater delusion nor catastrophe than to take this [heroic] view. For it would not be real nothingness [that the hero encounters], but only an ultimately innocuous counterfeit. . . . And while the creature is preoccupied with the assault and repulse of these counterfeits, it is already subject to the attack of real nothingness and its defence against it is already futile. In face of real nothingness the creature is already defeated and lost.[6]

Edgar may have defeated Edmund, but "real nothingness" has been left unscathed. Whatever it is that finds expression in insanity, human sin and natural storm will soon again disturb the fragile peace.

A fourth reading of nature is therefore suggested: that nature and whatever gods or demons may inhabit her unseen realms are indifferent to human moral theory, instruments only of a sovereign and destructive nothingness. Edmund is a fool for thinking that his imitation of nature's amorality would gain him nature's blessing. Lear is a fool for thinking that nature favors social order. And Edgar too is a fool unless he knows that his triumph over Edmund is a temporary aberration and

6. Barth, *CD,* 3/3, p. 358.

a distraction from the real and hopeless task of opposing true nothingness. In *King Lear,* the particular social conflicts between father and child, between legitimate ruler and usurper, are in some measure resolved. But to the conflict with nothingness which subsumes these particulars Shakespeare offers neither resolution nor hope of resolution.

Nietzsche and Grotowski

Nietzsche's *The Birth of Tragedy* begins where *King Lear* ends, and suggests that resolution may be found not in moral theory but in the theatrical event itself. In this respect, his most potent heir has been the Polish director, Jerzy Grotowski. Both begin by locating conflict, not in a clash between Good and Evil, but in a perceived distinction between subject and object, and both propose resolution through theatrical or, in the case of Grotowski's later work, "paratheatrical" rite. They differ most significantly, as we shall see, at the point where one embraces and the other assaults heroic myth.

In *The Birth of Tragedy,* Nietzsche scorns all rational stratagems to hold at bay the universal human terror at being alone in a fragmented and irrational world. Faith in an orderly universe, "the belief that man may plumb the universe by means of the law of causation" (18),[7] is, he declares, a sign of cultural senility, "the human mind terrified by pessimism and trying to escape from it, a clever bulwark erected against the truth" (A1). On the contrary, God is a kind of natural "process," a "supreme artist, amoral, recklessly creating and destroying," and all morality "an outrageous imposition" (A5).

To elude the "nausea" (7) that is often man's timid response to such irrationality, the Greeks invented "the shining fantasy of the Olympians," that mythical race of beautiful, superhuman gods who lived to the full "luxuriant, triumphant existence," untrammeled by hesitant morality. The Greek artists gave this dream form and hence a kind of reality. And "in the clear sunlight of such deities" the Greeks were able to rejoice; life was not absurd, for the gods "justified human

7. Quotations, from the Goiffing translation, are identified by numerical reference to the chapter divisions of *The Birth of Tragedy* and, when preceded by "A," to the chapters of Nietzsche's later preface, "A Critical Backward Glance."

life by living it themselves" without restraint and without shame (3). Such, for Nietzsche, was the achievement of "Apollonian" art.

But the universe is not only irrational; it is also fragmented. Nietzsche had inherited from the Romantic philosophers the conviction that "individuation is the root of all evil" (10); that, in Christian terms, Creation is Fall because "the original Oneness" (5) is thereby divided into Creator and creature; and that "nature" is ever since "bemoaning the fact of her fragmentation, her decomposition into separate individuals" (2). This problem Apollonian art could not solve unaided, for the dreamer remained alone. The solution of primitive peoples to this isolation had been "Dionysian"; at certain seasons "the individual [forgot] himself completely" (1) in communal rites. Unfortunately,

> the central concern of such celebrations was, almost universally, a complete sexual promiscuity overriding every form of established tribal law; all the savage urges of the mind were unleashed . . . until they reached [a] paroxysm of lust and cruelty (2).

Worshippers awoke from such an orgy with a kind of metaphysical hangover, their "mystical experience of the collective" (2) coming at the cost of a vivid reminder of the irrationality of the universe.

The genius of Greek tragedy, according to Nietzsche, was to combine the best of both worlds, the communal element of the Dionysian celebration and the saving vision of the Apollonian gods, in a single "esthetic event" (2). The spectators, already stimulated by the religious festival of which the tragedy was a part, envisioned themselves as a community of Dionysian revelers; their dream was given concrete form by the satyr chorus in the orchestra. The chorus in turn envisioned the gods, who were given form by the actors on stage. The spectators were thus transformed into joyous seers, entranced and united by their shared projection of the gods into concrete theatrical form. Claiming that "hope" for "the end of individuation . . . alone sheds a beam of joy on a ravaged and fragmented world" (10), Nietzsche called for the modern theatrical revival of such "rites of universal redemption, of glorious transfiguration" (2).

Nietzsche advocated, in short, the conquest of nothingness by a heroic act of the corporate imagination, summoning the ideal and unseen to provide a collective aesthetic escape from the messy (and often terrifying) experience of human time and space. Grotowski's work too may be viewed as a series of probes beneath the surface of theater and ritual to facilitate "meeting" and "to find a place where a communion becomes possible."[8] But Grotowski departs from Romantic tradition in his conviction that such communion is to be won by technical mastery and not by an act of the imagination. The heroic myths that appealed to Nietzsche are regarded by Grotowski as barriers to honest "encounter" and theatrically detonated with a single-minded ferocity.

Initially Grotowski focused on a triptych of meetings that include and take place either side of the essential theatrical encounter between actor and spectator. First there must be a meeting between the actor and the inner recesses of his own personality. Grotowski describes this as

> an extreme confrontation, sincere, disciplined, precise and total — not merely a confrontation with his thoughts, but one involving his whole being from his instincts and his unconscious right up to his most lucid states.[9]

Gradually the actor, under Grotowski's direction, learns "to eliminate his organism's resistance to this psychic process." He masters a technical vocabulary of sound and movement by which he is able, as if in a trance, to express directly every inner impulse, to lay bare all those "psychic and bodily powers which emerge from the most intimate layers of his being and his instinct."[10]

The fruit of this self-revelation is a second meeting between actor and spectator in which the latter's psychic defenses are penetrated and his consoling fantasies violated. For the actor to expose "the innermost part of himself" is in itself a violation of taboo. Still, in an age of skepticism, it is "difficult to elicit the sort of shock needed to get at those psychic layers behind the life mask" of the spectator. Grotowski therefore uses as a vehicle for the meeting between actor and audience a script which evokes archetypal images culled from "the collective complexes of society, . . . myths which are not an invention of the mind but

8. Grotowski, quoted in B. E. Clarke, "Grotowski Speaks Again," *Theater* (Spring 1982) p. 87.

9. J. Grotowski, *Towards a Poor Theatre* (New York: Touchstone, 1968) p. 57.

10. Ibid., p. 16.

are, so to speak, inherited through one's blood, religion, culture and climate."[11]

Such a text is Wyspianski's *Akropolis,* a patriotic classic of late Polish Romanticism. On the eve of Easter Sunday, in Krakow cathedral and on the battlements of the neighboring royal castle, statues and figures in tapestries come alive and enact heroic scenes from Polish history, from Homer's *Iliad* and from the biblical accounts of Jacob and Esau and of King David. The play ends with a triumphant and simultaneous resurrection of Christ and of Poland. Grotowski removed his adaptation of *Akropolis* from the patriotic background of cathedral and castle and set it instead in the concentration camp of Auschwitz, just 30 miles west of Krakow. The actors, uniformly dressed in ripped sackcloth, lined so as to suggest torn flesh, in heavy boots and drab cap, faces frozen in numbed grimaces and eyes dead, represent the victims of the camp, temporarily restored to life to re-enact their death.

From rusting scrap iron, the prisoners erect their crematorium; and during breaks in their work imagine themselves to be the heroes of Wyspianski's text. The prisoner who plays Jacob escorts Rachel, a length of stovepipe from which plastic wrapping hangs like a veil, in a wedding procession. Other prisoners follow, singing a Polish wedding song, and one rattles together two stage screws to indicate the chiming of church bells. Paris and Helen are both played by men. As they sit together, furtively uttering their declarations of love, the guards snicker. David demands to know when God will come for the salvation of his people and raises heavenwards a limp, headless dummy of a corpse, not the resurrected Christ but a starved and badly mauled victim of Gentile brutality in the concentration camp. To words taken from Wyspianski's triumphant ending and sung to the tune of a Polish carol, David leads the prisoners in a last procession to their death in the crematorium. The audience sits in silence, usually shaken beyond the possibility of applause.[12]

The encounter between actors and audience on such an occasion entails an implicit invitation to the spectator to embark on a third meeting, this time with himself. The myths that usually conceal his deepest fears and longings have been blasphemed, and he is now in a

11. Ibid., pp. 23, 42.

12. R. Findlay, "Grotowski's *Akropolos:* A Retrospective View," *Modern Drama* 27 (March 1984) pp. 1-20.

position to meet himself truly, in a manner modeled for him by the self-exposure of the actor. Such an encounter, Grotowski believed, was therapeutic, leading "to a liberation from complexes in much the same way as psycho-analytic therapy," such that the spectator who truly participates "leaves the theatre in a state of greater inner harmony."[13]

The "plot" of Grotowski's *Akropolis* lies as much in this triptych of "encounters" as it does in the internal narrative of the text. Tzvetan Todorov has written that "the minimal complete plot consists in the passage from one equilibrium to another" through an intervening "disequilibrium."[14] In *Akropolis,* actors who have learned to lay themselves bare confront spectators who are presumed to be hiding. The initial equilibrium of *Akropolis,* therefore, is that of the spectators, a false peace to be deliberately disturbed by the performance. "We create," Grotowski said, "the conditions for a brutal confrontation between the spectator and the myth"[15] and thus the performance "engages in a sort of psychic conflict with the spectator." "Disequilibrium" is the immediate consequence of this assault: "all the standards [the spectator] is used to trusting must suddenly fail him."[16] But, if the performance succeeds, the spectator who is in "a state of grace"[17] is granted an "inner harmony" possible only to those who have passed through such an ordeal. Contrary to Todorov, therefore, this "second equilibrium" is not "similar to the first," but qualitatively different: the first was founded on deception, the second on disclosure.

By 1970, however, Grotowski had decided that this theater of derision could not in fact heal. After the stripping of the myths, there remained, in human terms, only a devastating "lack of meaning," and, in theatrical terms, the unresolved division of performer and audience. And so, "leaving theatre behind," he turned to "paratheatrical" projects, aimed at generating "holiday" or "the day that is holy," occasions for the discovery of "brotherhood" not only between man and man but also between man and nature:

13. Grotowski, op. cit., p. 46.

14. Todorov, op. cit., p. 111.

15. Grotowski, op. cit., p. 47.

16. Grotowski, quoted in E. Barba and L. Flaszen, "A Theatre of Magic and Sacrilege," *Tulane Drama Review,* Vol. 9, no. 3 (Spring 1965) p. 186.

17. Grotowski, quoted in Z. Osiński, *Grotowski and his Laboratory,* trans. L. Vallee and R. Findlay (New York: PAJ Publications, 1986) p. 171; cf. p. 85.

> Brother . . . contains "the likeness of God," giving and man; but also the brother of earth, the brother of senses, the brother of sun, the brother of touch, the brother of Milky Way, the brother of grass, the brother of river.[18]

Between 1970 and 1975 members of Grotowski's *Teatr Laboratorium* led invited participants from the world of theater through prepared encounters with water, earth, air and fire. One participant remembers "lakes, brooks, shaky bridges over rapid streams, and endless pools of water" that had to be passed, "columns of fire" that "lined the path as the group arched its way through the woods," and "glowing coals" that the group blew on to send "shimmering white sparks up to the heavens."[19] Another recalls how, for several hours

> we walked and ran [barefoot] through the woods, and waded through the streams, ran through the fields with chest-high grass under a full moon, . . . got baptized in a hole full of water, crawled like frogs,

emerging finally in a clearing where "for hours we danced around the fire." "By the end," he remembers,

> I felt a profound connection with the natural world. . . . One of my most memorable moments was when I found myself digging with my hands into the loose earth of a recently plowed field full of roots and asking the roots who I was.[20]

Reading of these projects, one is struck by the idea that Grotowski is trying to craft therapy from the raw material of Poor Tom's nocturnal wanderings. Benign fairies, however, lead rustics and lovers on a similar journey in *A Midsummer Night's Dream,* and do so to their humbling and not their harm. Grotowski's aim is simply to create an environment in which "real meeting" may take place.

18. Grotowski, "Holiday: The Day That Is Holy," *The Drama Review,* vol. 17, no. 2 (June 1973) p. 119.

19. M. Croyden, "New theater rule: no watching allowed," *Vogue* (December 1975) pp. 196-97.

20. R. Mennen, "Jerzy Grotowski's Paratheatrical Projects," *The Drama Review,* Vol. 19, no. 4 (December 1975) pp. 58-69.

Such "participatory theatre," however, demands "mastery" and not "dilettantism," for "banalities exist in participatory theatre as well as in classical theatre." It is all too easy to start "acting the part of 'savages,' imitating trances, . . . creating processions, . . . presenting personal behavioral cliches as improvisations." Aware of this danger, Grotowski began to realize that

> in certain traditional human activities – which may be called religious – from different cultures where tradition still existed, it was possible to see, in some places, participatory theatre without banality.[21]

Most recently, therefore, Grotowski has worked at what he has successively called "The Theatre of Sources" and "Objective Drama." Bringing together "traditional practitioners" from a wide variety of theatrical and ritual cultures – Haitian voodoo, Sufi whirling, Buddhist incantation, sacred Bengali dance and song – he has sought to isolate those elements in traditional ritual and performance "which have a precise, and therefore objective, impact on participants, quite apart from solely theological or symbolical significance,"[22] hoping thereby to discover ways of moving and of vocalizing that "deobjectify one's world," allowing "earth, sky, foliage, animal and 'other' to appear as subjects."[23]

It is perhaps too early to assess the value of Grotowski's work since 1970. Whether it will give birth, as he hopes, to a "new art," or whether, as some suspect, the interest he continues to generate is due not to the quality of his current research but to the undoubted brilliance of his work as a director in the 1960s, remains to be seen. In any case, both his theatrical and "post-theatrical" work can be understood as part of a single, evolving project, addressing the problem of conflict that Grotowski believes to be grounded in individuation and the hope of resolution that he believes to be offered by an unmediated "aware[ness] of the indivisible unity of nature,"[24] humanity included. In neither case does the prepared event point to the means of resolution, as, for example, a Cor-

21. Grotowski, "Tu es le fils de quelqu'un," *The Drama Review,* vol. 31, no. 3 (Autumn 1987) pp. 32-33.

22. Quoted by Findlay in Osiński, op. cit., p. 173.

23. R. Grimes, "The Theatre of Sources," *The Drama Review* (Autumn 1981) p. 69.

24. Quoted in Osiński, op. cit., p. 27.

pus Christi play did; instead, it is offered as itself the means of resolution. Put another way, it aspires to effect resolution, in the manner of ritual, rather than to imitate resolution, in the manner of play.

Christ and the "Conflict with Nothingness"

For all that Nietzsche scorns a heroism that manifests itself in allegiance to duty and Grotowski rejects the exuberance of Nietzsche's mythic heroes, both remain, by Barth's definition, "heroes," convinced that it is possible for man to "suffer and fight and finally conquer this adversary" of nothingness, either by imagining a new world into being through theatrical art or by uncovering techniques by which subject and object may at last be reunited. It is worth, therefore, looking again at a play in which no such claim is made and, in that context, at Barth's proposal that the "conflict with nothingness" has already been resolved.

In *The Castle of Perseverance,* Mankind is no hero; he is a recipient of grace. In this play, to use Barth's terms, "nothingness" takes the "form of sin, evil [and] death" and the consequent terror of God's "wrath and judgment."[25] But Mankind's failure does not signal defeat in the conflict with nothingness. Christ's virtues have battled with demonic vices both for and through him, and though he walks away from the battle in old age, at death he entrusts himself once more to God's mercy (3007). The four daughters of God – Truth, Mercy, Peace and Righteousness – debate the outcome of the drama. Truth and Righteousness demand that Mankind remain under condemnation; Peace and Mercy recall the death of Christ, where, in Barth's words, "the true conflict with nothingness took place."[26] God rules unhesitatingly in favor of Mercy, and Mankind's soul is welcomed to heaven. "Full well have I loved thee," God reassures him, "Unkind though I thee found" (3600-3601).

Unlike the Corpus Christi plays, *The Castle of Perseverance* contains no Last Judgement. The resolution displays instead the unqualified triumph of mercy over nothingness: no man is damned and Mankind in

25. Barth, *CD,* 3/3, pp. 354, 357.
26. Ibid., p. 360.

his entirety is seated at the right hand of God. This entailed no challenge to orthodoxy. If the life of a single representative Mankind were to be played, he must be either damned or saved, and, in the history of the theater, it was not until Marlowe's *Doctor Faustus* that judgement triumphed over grace. In *The Castle of Perseverance,* though the possibility of judgement is present, it is not played, and this must have made for a particularly joyous singing of the corporate *Te Deum* at the close of performance.

Barth would have approved:

> What is nothingness? In the knowledge and confession of the Christian faith, i.e., looking retrospectively to the resurrection of Jesus Christ and prospectively to His coming again, there is only one possible answer. Nothingness is the past, the ancient menace, danger and destruction, the ancient non-being which obscured and defaced the divine creation of God but which is consigned to the past in Jesus Christ, in whose death it has received its deserts. . . . Because Jesus is Victor, nothingness is routed and extirpated. . . . This is its status and appearance now that God has made His own and carried through the conflict with it in His Son.[27]

Barth can make this claim because he believes that real nothingness cannot be known, let alone defeated, apart from God's self-revelation in Christ. But, known in this way, it is known as already vanquished. Real nothingness is no more nor less than "that which brought Christ to the cross, and that which He defeated there." There alone but there decisively "the true conflict with nothingness [took] place," and nothingness proved "impotent," unable to "master this victim. It could neither endure nor bear the presence of God in the flesh."[28]

It follows that "the controversy with nothingness, its conquest, removal and abolition are primarily and properly God's own affair" and not man's. God has in Christ taken upon himself man's conflict with nothingness and made it his own. "Though Adam is fallen and disgraced, he is not too low for God to make Himself his Brother," and in love to contend for him. This being the case, it is always "a decision

27. Ibid., p. 363.
28. Ibid., pp. 305, 362.

against the grace of God," a submission to the myths of human heroism, for man to oppose nothingness alone. It is the delusion of the hero to believe that he can and of the desperate man to believe that he must. Both, rather than resist nothingness, in fact embody it. For "it is God's honour and right to be gracious, and this is what nothingness contests." What the hero fights and the desperate person fears, in other words, is only a counterfeit of nothingness; real nothingness is their own refusal of grace. "There are few heresies so pernicious," Barth concludes, "as that of a God who faces nothingness more or less unaffected and unconcerned, and the parallel doctrine of man as one who must engage in independent conflict against it."[29]

One wonders if, at this point, Barth has in mind the Stoic concept of the wise man in conflict with fate being a spectacle [θέατρον] for gods and men. Kittel comments, "In the Stoic use [of the theatrical image] deity is a spectator of the battle which man himself fights in the proud autonomy of his heroism." Kittel contrasts this with the Pauline use of the word in 1 Cor. 4:9, where "God is the author of the weakness of His apostles," which is, therefore, paradoxically, "true . . . power." Thus "what is really enacted" in the apostolic θέατρον is not "a sorry . . . and contemptible" defeat but the grace of God at work in the weakness of his servants.[30] Barth writes:

> It is not in the vacuum of creaturely self-sufficiency but under the wings of divine mercy that the fortitude thrives in which man is summoned and equipped to range himself with God, so that in his own place he opposes nothingness and thus has a part in the work and warfare of God.[31]

For Barth, it is not in heroism but in acknowledged weakness, finding courage in the mercy of God, that man may work alongside God in true opposition to the residue of a defeated nothingness.

29. Ibid., pp. 354, 357, 358, 353, 360.
30. G. Kittel, "θέατρον," *Theological Dictionary of the New Testament,* III, p. 43.
31. Barth, *CD,* 3/3, p. 359.

A Midsummer Night's Dream

Barth's good friend and fellow theologian, Heinrich Vogel, has written of "the laughing Barth," his good humor grounded in the faith that "all will end well in God's purposes in Jesus Christ."[32] Barth's conviction that history, like comedy, will end well and that, in the meanwhile, human beings should not camouflage their weakness with heroism points us to an alternative view of conflict and resolution: the comic.

When, in Shakespeare's *A Midsummer Night's Dream,* Bottom emerges from the bushes, sporting an ass's head, Master Quince and his "crew of . . . rude mechanicals" scatter like panic-stricken birds before a hunter's gun (III, ii). The audience roars with laughter and Puck boasts:

> I'll follow you; I'll lead you about a round,
> Through bog, through bush, through brake, through brier;
> Sometime a horse I'll be, sometime a hound,
> A hog, a headless bear, sometime a fire;
> And neigh, and bark, and grunt, and roar, and burn,
> Like horse, hound, hog, bear, fire, at every turn. (III, i)

William Lynch regards this third nocturnal tour of the elements "as a miniature essay on the problem of disgust" masquerading as comedy. Puck, he writes, "is a dubious comic spirit, . . . intent on transforming the human" into something "monstrous," provoking "the laughter of the disgusted man." True comedy, on the other hand, is a "defender" of the "human order," in all its muddiness and actuality and freedom, a resistance to any "hankering for divine power."[33]

Lynch may well be right about comedy, but I believe he is mistaken in his reading of *A Midsummer Night's Dream.* Puck's celebrated opinion, "Lord, what fools these mortals be" (III, ii), is a judgement not on humanity as such but on humanity's pretensions. Remember the context of Bottom's transformation. The craftsmen are rehearsing "the

32. H. Vogel, "Der lachende Barth," in *Antwort: Karl Barth zum Siebzigsten Geburtstag am 10 Mai 1956,* ed. E. Wolf, C. von Kirschbaum and R. Frey (Zollikon-Zurich: Evangelischer Verlag, 1956) pp. 64-171; cited in B. Ramm, *After Fundamentalism* (San Francisco: Harper & Row, 1983) p. 195.

33. Lynch, op. cit., pp. 103-4, 107.

most lamentable comedy, and most cruel death of Pyramus and Thisby," in which Pyramus "kills himself most gallantly for love." All aspire to a kind of exaltation, playing heroic roles before royalty. Of Bottom especially this is true. He plays the hero, Pyramus, and if he could would play the heroine, the roaring lion, and the "tyrant" Hercules as well. He would replace Quince as director, controlling the production so as neither to confuse nor frighten the ladies among the royal audience and demanding of the company perfection ("Take pains; be perfect") (I, ii). In advance parody of Oberon's supernatural confidence that "all things shall be peace," echoed by Puck ("All shall be well") (III, ii), Bottom boasts, "I have a device to make all well" (III, i). Bottom, then, would be a hero, allaying the fear of ladies, killing lions, sacrificing himself on the altar of love, controlling his companions and making all things well. His transformation, showing him to be, in all his pretensions to heroism, an "ass"; the instant fear of the other "heroic" actors; the roundabout chase "through bog, through bush, through brake, through brier," in which spirits are nimble and humans clumsy; all these function, in the economy of the play, not to inspire disgust but to humble "heroes" to humans.

The same is true of Puck's sport with the lovers. Like Pyramus and Thisbe, they aspire to heroism in the field of romance. Though they observe convention, sending "rhymes," exchanging "love-tokens," singing by moonlight at the lover's window, proclaiming a nunnery preferable to a forced marriage and, secretly, elopement better yet, they deny (again observing convention) that they could ever suffer the weakness of other lovers, confidently swearing fidelity "by all the vows that ever men have broke" (I, i). The confusion that follows Puck's misapplication of the love potion does not invite disgust so much as delight in the caricature of fickleness that it juxtaposes to the lovers' superhuman aspirations. They are humbled, not because humanity is to be despised, but because humanity is to be affirmed and the lovers' claim to have risen above human weakness refuses to do that.

Demetrius, waking under the influence of the love-juice, extols Helen's beauty. She is a "goddess, nymph, perfect divine!" Compared to her sparkling eyes, even "crystal is muddy" (III, ii). But sleeping "on the dank and dirty ground" (II, iii), led astray through bog and bush and "drooping fog," "bedabbled with dew and torn with briers" (III, ii), the lovers by morning are weary, human and muddy, earthenware not crystal. Lynch, in his discussion of comedy, makes much of man being "muddy." It is "the mud of detail" in which humanity is mired that challenges our pretensions to transcendence. "The mud in man . . . is nothing to be ashamed of. It can produce" – in the Incarnation and, to the degree that Christ's light shines in our humanity, in us too – "the face of God. To recall this, to recall this incredible relationship between mud and God, is, in its own distant, adumbrating way, the function of comedy."[34] In *A Midsummer Night's Dream,* the aspirations of humanity to be something more than human are, quite literally, dragged through the mud.

If Lynch is correct, the conflict of comedy, though it may find expression in many and various social and romantic clashes, in mistaken identity or pratfalls, is finally one between human overreaching and human finitude. The comic resolution is one in which "all shall be well," not simply because lovers are reunited or heirs properly identified, but because there is no fundamental dichotomy, with respect to our humanness, between what we are and what we ought to be.

Such a resolution in the theater need not be grounded in a Christian faith. *A Midsummer Night's Dream* affirms only that the "gods" (or fairies), though mischievous, are not opposed to our humanity but only to our pretensions to be more than human. It is well to be human. But Christianity declares as much and more. As Nathan Scott points out, "the great sympathy which the Christian imagination may feel for the testimony of the comedian"[35] is, in large part, due to the affirmation of humanity that lies at the heart of the Christian faith. The doctrines of Creation and Incarnation, declaring both that "God saw everything that he had made, and behold, it was very good," and that God became human flesh and blood, contain and limit the doctrine of sin, into which humanity fell and in the midst of which grace befriends us:

> The Christian's fundamental attitude toward existence must always be profoundly affirmative: the particularity and fragmentariness of existence can never be, for him, the offense that they are to more fastidious men: nor can he ever in any way impugn the validity of the natural and the temporal order, since [this was made by

34. Ibid., pp. 107, 109.
35. Scott, *The Broken Center,* p. 109.

> God] and for approximately thirty years . . . was the home of God Himself.[36]

One could well add to these doctrines Barth's insistence that "the ancient menace," that "nothingness" which man fears and attempts to identify and oppose, has been decisively defeated, "once for all," in Christ. Not knowing this, we may be tempted to play the tragic hero, arming ourselves against a counterfeit nothingness, hoping against hope that we might close the door on darkness or find the key that will release the flood of light, and yet deep down fearing that humankind is in an interminable conflict that brooks no resolution. Knowing that Christ is Victor, we may still in all seriousness and to exhaustion resist the lingering shadows of nothingness, but we will do so not as heroes but as human beings, mudstained and capable of laughter, trusting in the great comic anthem, "All shall be well, and all shall be well, and all manner of thing shall be well."[37]

36. Ibid., p. 115.

37. Julian of Norwich, *Revelations of Divine Love,* ch. 27, ed. G. Warwick (London: Methuen, 1901) p. 56.

Index